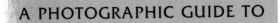
A PHOTOGRAPHIC GUIDE TO
BUTTERFLIES
BRITAIN
AND EUROPE

PAUL STERRY

This edition published in 2001 by
New Holland Publishers (UK) Ltd
London • Cape Town • Sydney • Auckland

Garfield House   80 McKenzie Street   14 Aquatic Drive
86 Edgware Road   Cape Town 8001   Frenchs Forest, NSW 2086
London W2 2EA   South Africa   Australia

First published in 1995

ISBN 1 85974 730 2

Editor: Charlie Fox
Designed and typeset by D & N Publishing, Hungerford, Berkshire.

Reproduction by Daylight Colour Arts (Pte) Ltd, Singapore
Printed and bound in Malaysia by Times Offset (M) Sdn Bhd

10 9 8 7 6 5 4 3

Front cover photograph: Purple Emperor (Paul Sterry)
Back cover photograph: Small Copper (Paul Sterry)
Title page photograph: Clouded Yellow (Paul Sterry)

Photographic acknowledgements
The majority of the photographs were supplied through Nature Photographers
Ltd. Many were taken by the author, the exceptions being:
Nature Photographers Ltd: SC Bisserot 19l, 29u, 39u, 44u, 45l, 66u, 70u,
115l, 116u, 117u, 119l; Ken Blamire 23l, 27l, 38u, 53l, 54l, 55l, 57u, 57l,
58l, 63l, 67l, 69l, 71l, 74u, 77l, 79u, 79l, 82u, 82m, 84u, 84l, 85u, 88u, 97l,
104l, 107l; Robin Bush 14u, 17lr, 18l, 21u, 25u, 25l, 34u, 35m, 40u, 40m,
46u, 75u, 80l, 85lr, 100l; NA Callow 41u, 62l, 83l, 95u, 99l, 105u, 108u;
Kevin Carlson 15u, 22l, 24u, 30l, 47l, 48u, 50u, 51u, 87u, 91u, 91l, 101l,
117l; Andrew Cleave 50lr, 97u, 129u; Geoff du Feu 36l; Michael Gore 29l;
LG Jessup 39m, 89l; Roger Tidman 116l; Anthony Wharton 32l, 40l, 42l,
105l.
Other sources of photographs were as follows:
Archmain Ltd: Dr Jim Asher 28l, 31l, 37l, 43u, 48l, 53u, 56u, 58u, 68u, 88l,
92u, 92l, 96u, 96l, 99u, 103u, 106l; Greg Herbert 16u, 26l, 71u, 83u, 98u,
106u; Tony Hoare 18u, 21l, 26u, 33u, 34l, 41u, 46l, 49u, 51l, 55u, 60u, 60l,
61u, 61l, 62u, 63u, 70l, 72u, 74l, 78l, 81l, 82l, 86u, 90l, 93l, 95l, 98l, 100u,
101u, 103l, 104u; T Munns 94l.
Natural Image: Jean Hall 102l; Alec Harmer 90u; Peter Wilson 16l, 20u,
89u.
Wildlife Matters: 30u, 42u, 44l, 52u, 54l, 56l, 64u, 64l.
u = upper, l = lower, m = middle, lr = lower right.

The author would like to thank Gary Roberts of Archmain Ltd for his help

Contents

Introduction

Butterflies contribute to most people's enjoyment of the countryside. During the warm, summer months, when most European species are on the wing, these active insects are encountered on walks almost everywhere, sharing the rambling naturalist's love of sunny weather. Most people are aware of a few species that they commonly encounter. However, by taking a greater interest in the subject, visiting different habitats and regions, and acquiring the ability to identify species with certainty, a whole new field of natural history interest can be opened up.

Once you have developed a taste for butterfly watching, you will soon realize that, as a pastime, it is far from restricted to lowland hedgerow habitats or your garden, or, for that matter, to the summer months alone. Butterflies occur in almost every conceivable land-based habitat in Europe, from sea-level up to the snow-line, and different species can be seen flying from March right through to October. Add to this the study of butterfly life-cycles and an interest in moths, and the naturalist can be occupied year-round with these amazing insects.

There are about 68 species of butterfly on the British list but in the whole of Europe, the region covered by this book, there are more than 360 species. Although some butterflies are widespread, many are surprisingly restricted in their range. It was felt appropriate, therefore, to restrict the number of butterfly species in this book to around 200, comprising the commonest and most widespread, as well as some of the more distinctive or spectacular local butterflies. In view of the potential confusion of some day-flying moths with butterflies, it was also felt appropriate to include several of these species together with some of the larger and more stunning nocturnal moths that are sometimes encountered resting during the daytime.

The distribution mentioned in the text for each species refers to mainland regions of Europe rather than offshore islands, which tend to have a smaller range of species than adjacent areas of mainland. Information on specific island butterfly fauna may be partially available in some of the more comprehensive books, but often has to be researched by one's own efforts, work that can be very interesting and rewarding in its own right.

How to use this book

The bulk of this book is devoted to species descriptions. Each butterfly or moth is illustrated with one or more photographs accompanied by informative text to help identify the species in question and provide background information. The species are arranged according to families and in an order that follows the convention of most other guides to butterflies and moths.

The photographs

For all the species included in this book as main descriptions, at least one colour photograph is included. The illustration of these species does pose problems for a book of this size, since butterflies often have startlingly different uppersides and undersides and very often the sexes have differing markings or colours too. In all cases, the photograph judged to be the most useful for identification has been chosen. In many cases, the photographs show males rather than females where there is a sex difference, as these often offer the best chances of a successful identification. The upperwings have been shown in preference to the underwings unless the latter provide more useful clues for identification. For example, in the case of most grayling species, the upperwings are almost never seen when the insect is resting.

The descriptions

The descriptions provide detailed information about each species. They have been written to complement the information conveyed by the photographs and to enable identification of the species when seen from another view or even a different sex. Where possible, the order in which the information is presented is consistent throughout each description, thus enabling comparisons between butterflies to be made more easily.

The first entry in the description is the popular, or common name which is printed in bold. Only one of the species mentioned in this book (a moth) has no common name in English. The scientific name comes next and is printed in italics. Although the common name will obviously vary from country to country and between languages, the scientific name remains constant and therefore provides an effective means of communication between butterfly enthusiasts anywhere in the world. A cautionary note should be sounded here, however. Butterfly taxonomists are forever debating and refining the classification of European species. Some scientific names will have changed from those given in earlier books on the subject. The English names are, however, long-established and will not be different.

The next entry refers to the wingspan of the butterfly or moth in millimetres (mm) with its wings spread. For obvious reasons, this is not a measurement that can be easily verified in the field with active species. It does, however, serve a useful purpose when studying captive or resting individuals, or when making species size comparisons. For those species who normally rest with their wings folded, the measurements are still given for spread wings; these should be halved where appropriate.

In the species descriptions, the order of the text in most cases follows a standard sequence. Following the summary sentence at the start are descriptions of the upperwings and then the underwings; colours and distinctive markings are highlighted. Next comes the species European range with mention given of its presence or absence in specific regions such as Britain, Scandinavia or Iberia. The flying season, which can often give vital identification clues, is then given followed by habitat preferences, altitude of occurrence where relevant, habits and larval foodplants.

Corner tabs
These provide an at-a-glance reference relating to the species family groups. See key below.

 Swallowtails

 Festoons & Apollos

 Whites & Orange Tips

 African Migrant & Clouded Yellows

 Brimstone & Cleopatra

 Wood Whites

 Monarchs

 Nymphalid family

 Fritillaries

 Marbled Whites

 Graylings & Hermits

 Satyrs, other Graylings & Ringlets

 Meadow Brown, Gate-keepers & Heaths

 Speckled Woods & other Browns

 Duke of Burgundy Fritillary

 Hairstreaks

 Coppers

 Long- & Short-tailed Blues

 Silver-studded Blue & allies

 Chalk-hill Blue & allies

 Common Blue & allies

 Grizzled Skippers & allies

 Chequered Skippers

 Large Skipper & allies

 Hawk Moths

 Prominents, Lutestrings & Yellow-tail

 Lackeys & Lappets

Emperor Moth

Garden Tiger & allies

Silver Y & allies

6

The butterfly life cycle

Butterflies and moths have a life cycle which involves four distinct stages and these are the egg, larva (or caterpillar), pupa (or chrysalis) and adult. These insects are described as having complete metamorphosis.

The egg

Eggs may be laid singly, in small groups or in batches, depending on the habits of the species. All are small but visible to the naked eye; with a hand-lens or binocular microscope, a great deal of attractive sculpturing is revealed on their surfaces. Each species lays eggs that are individual in shape, pattern and colour, although the characteristics of a family may be observed from the egg. For example, the whites lay eggs that are tall and bottle-shaped while the coppers lay eggs that are round.

The duration of the egg stage is dependent upon temperature and varies with the species. A typical time would be from two to three weeks, but there are species that overwinter as eggs, staying in the egg from summer through to the following spring.

The outer shell of the egg is rigid, sometimes hard. There is a central closed orifice, the micropyle, through which the egg is fertilized in the female's abdomen and through which the developing larva breathes. Once the larva is fully formed, its mandibles are strong enough to pierce the eggshell and a hole is eaten just large enough to allow the larva to emerge through.

The larva

Larvae grow continuously and may become a thousand times their original size and weight; their main purpose is to eat and grow. Although their skin is elastic, it could not possibly accommodate this dramatic increase in size during a larva's life. To solve this problem, the skin is shed at intervals to reveal a new skin beneath, each new one being much larger than the previous one. There are usually at least four skin changes and the periods between them are known as instars.

As with eggs and adults of butterflies and moths, larvae are unique in their colouring, shape and pattern, although there are often similarities between closely related species. Some larvae are solitary while others are gregarious.

Larvae are vulnerable to attack by predators and are often well camouflaged to blend in with their foodplant or location. Frequently they are hidden by day and only stir to feed under cover of darkness. A few have irritating hairs to deter attack while a small number are poisonous and use warning colours to advertise the fact.

The larval stage usually lasts from one to two months but, as with the other stages, this is dependent on temperature and species. There are many larvae that hibernate; their lives, therefore, can be nine or ten months.

The pupa

The change from active larva to static pupa or chrysalis is one of nature's great wonders. At the end of the final instar (the fifth in most species) there is one more skin change. The skin splits to reveal a glistening wet creature with the appearance of a hunched-up larva. After a few hours, or even a day, the pupal characters become pronounced and the outer layer dries and hardens; the pupal stage is then fully formed.

Before this final transformation, the larva seeks a place in which to pupate. Butterfly larvae almost never spin a cocoon and so need to find a concealed spot where the immobile pupa will be safe from predation. Some are suspended by the tail, hanging free with the head downwards. Others employ a belt and braces approach being attached at the tail end although not suspended, and with a girdle of silk around the junction of the thorax and abdomen; this sling holds the pupa, head upwards, against a stem. A third approach is adopted by pupae that lie loose or enveloped in silk. Many moth pupae are enclosed by silk cocoons but this is not the case with most butterflies. Skipper butterflies make a loose tent of grass blades and silk in which to pupate.

Inside the newly formed pupal case there is much activity. At first, the main contents comprise essential organs immersed in blood. From the minute beginnings of adult features, cells grow to produce the recognizable adult characters.

The adult

The adult can be seen forming inside the pupal case in the last days before it is ready to emerge. The last signs are the bright colours which show through the wing cases. When it is ready to emerge, the adult breaks open the pupal case, pulls itself out and seeks a place where it can hang and expand its wings by pumping blood into them. The expansion of the wings is almost fast enough to observe, and the full length is achieved in approximately twenty minutes.

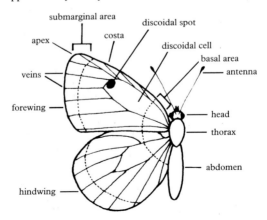

The wings are very soft and floppy for about an hour and the insect is vulnerable at this stage if found by a predator. Once the wings are dry, the butterfly or moth is ready to fly and begin its life in search of nectar and a mate. The life of the adult may be as short as a few days, just enough time to breed; but in the case of some species, the adult may live for weeks or even months, perhaps overwintering.

Butterfly and moth structure

All species of butterflies and moths have two pairs of wings and most are able to perform active and often rapid flight. Exceptions to this rule are found in a few species of moths where the females have vestigial wings and are incapable of flight. In most species, the wings are covered in coloured scales on both the upper and lower surfaces; these may be lost with wear.

Rigidity of the wings is provided by a network of veins. These form regular patterns, with the spaces between veins referred to as 'cells', to which taxonomists often refer when distinguishing species; the discoidal cell on the forewing often contains an area with markings particularly useful for identification.

The males of some species of butterfly have upperwings that bear scent brands. Sometimes referred to as sex brands, they are marks or patches of scent-scales which contain pheromones (chemicals associated with sexual attraction), essential to courtship. Not all butterflies have scent brands but they are important to those that do, such as certain species of hairstreaks, like the Green Hairstreak, which has a small oval patch close to the leading edge of the forewing. Many of the browns have scent scales covering quite large areas of the forewing and some of the skippers have scent brands forming an oblique slash mark.

In common with all insects, a butterfly or moth's body comprises three main sections: head, thorax and abdomen. The head bears the eyes, mouthparts and antennae, and the thorax the three pairs of legs and two pairs of wings; the abdomen is segmented and contains many of the insect's vital organs.

At first glance, the distinction between butterflies and moths may seem rather arbitrary. Butterflies are invariably day-flying insects while moths are, on the whole, nocturnal. There are, however, many day-flying moths that could pass for butterflies superficially and it is among these that confusion can occur. Distinguishing features to look at include the antennae which are club-tipped or swollen-tipped in butterflies; in moths, they are filamentous or feathery depending on the species and sex. At rest, most butterflies hold their wings folded vertically over their bodies while resting moths have their wings flat, the forewings usually covering the hindwings. There are exceptions to even this rule, however, for example among the skipper butterflies, members of which often rest in moth-like pose and in thorn moths, which often rest with wings folded like butterflies.

Studying butterflies and moths

The study of butterflies and moths can be an immensely rewarding pastime. Not only are the insects themselves attractive to look at but they are often found in beautiful settings. The first thing you will wish to master is the identification of the common species that you encounter. Using the text and photographs in this book, and with a degree of patience and persistence, you should eventually become proficient in this field. However, there are several factors that should be borne in mind which can greatly increase your chances of getting a good view of the butterfly or moth, studying it closely and hence identifying it with certainty.

Most species of butterflies are sun-loving insects, and only active when the sun is shining. Try visiting an area of grassland early in the morning, before the heat of the sun has fully warmed the cool air. You are likely to encounter blue butterflies sitting around on grass and flower heads, either in their overnight resting posture or warming up in the sun with their wings open. They are usually docile and easily approached then and behave in a similar way as evening approaches too. This same sluggish, early-morning behaviour can be seen in many of the fritillaries including Marsh Fritillary and Heath Fritillary; it tends to take them up to half an hour to get going in the mornings!

Studying some of the upland brown butterflies can be a rather frustrating business because they are often active in sunny weather and get carried by gusts of wind faster than you can follow them. Species such as the Small Mountain Ringlet have extremely sun-dependent activity levels, dropping like a stone into the grass the moment the sun disappears behind a cloud. Visit their habitat on a partly cloudy day and use their behaviour to your advantage. Watch where they drop when the sun goes in and then search for them; having found them, wait until the sun reappears and you will have a few seconds to see them warming up with their wings open.

The adult butterfly's sole purpose in life is to reproduce and this necessarily occupies its time to the exclusion of almost all other activities except staying alive long enough to do so. Mating and egg-laying butterflies are often so preoccupied or otherwise engaged that they can be observed more easily than other individuals. Mating pairs often fly around in tandem for a while; although they can be approached and studied, they should not be disturbed because this may result in the couple separating prematurely.

Feeding and drinking butterflies also offer excellent opportunities for close study. Many species, however, are extremely wary and a more patient approach may be needed. If you want to observe Dark Green Fritillaries, for example, try sitting motionless beside a clump of flowers of Great Knapweed on a suitable area of downland and simply wait. Marbled Whites and skippers will soon visit and eventually one of these magnificent butterflies will also come. The same wait-and-see approach works well with wary woodland butterflies, such as White Admirals which are fond of visiting Bramble flowers. The Purple Emperor, however, requires an altogether more dedicated and single-minded butterfly watcher: their predilection is for manure and rotting carcasses.

Night-flying species of moths can be searched for while they are resting during the daytime among foliage and on tree trunks. However, many naturalists increase their chances of observation by tackling these insects after dark. You only have to switch on an outside light during the summer months to know that moths are attracted to light. They are particularly receptive to ultra-violet rays and traps with mercury vapour lamps can be purchased or built specifically for the purpose. The traps do not kill the moths but simply keep them contained until they can be studied in the morning. Moths' other great weakness is for sugary fluids, and some moth enthusiasts paint fences and tree trunks with a mixture of treacle, honey and rum to attract them. The method works best on warm, muggy evenings, and is perhaps most enjoyable if the moth-watcher partakes of the brew as well!

Breeding butterflies and moths

Breeding butterflies and moths can bring much pleasure and greatly add to your knowledge. The larvae can be found in the wild or bought from suppliers. If collecting from the field, do not take a mass of larvae if they are gregarious; collect just enough to maintain their gregarious habit but leave the rest remaining wild.

One of the best species to start with is the Small Tortoiseshell. It is quite common and lives in colonies, so it is not harmful to take a few. The total life of the larva is about a month, so wild-collected ones may pupate in as little as a fortnight and, with a pupal period of barely two weeks, the butterflies will emerge often in less than a month from the start of rearing.

If rearing this or any other larva from the wild, remember to use the foodplant on which it was found. If this fails, experiment with various plants but return the larva to where it was found if it does not feed in the first day.

If you choose to rear the larvae on potted foodplants, enclose the plant in netting to prevent the larvae escaping and parasitic wasps from attacking them. An alternative method of rearing is in clear, transparent plastic boxes, on cut foodplants. Line the box with absorbent paper and change the food and empty the droppings on a daily basis, using a fine paintbrush to move the larvae. Never use wet plant material and never stand the box in the sun. Make sure you know about the life-cycle of the insect in question: some will pupate in the same year while others may hibernate as larvae.

Larger larvae should be kept in a cage prior to pupation. A wooden-framed netting cage is suitable; parasitic wasps can be a problem if the mesh of the netting is not fine enough. Butterflies will usually pupate either among the foodplant or on the floor of the cage; moth larvae often burrow underground to pupate and so a tray of soil should be placed on the floor of the cage. Try not to disturb a pupa for at least one week because it will be vulnerable to damage. You should also find out whether the species in question will emerge in the same year or whether it passes the winter as a pupa.

Photography

Thankfully, for most butterfly and moth enthusiasts, gone are the days when they went into the field armed with a net and killing jar, collecting specimens to stock dusty cabinet drawers. Watching these amazing insects in the wild is often reward enough in itself but some people choose to record their sightings on film. For the beginner butterfly watcher, photographing butterflies can be an excellent way of learning to identify the common species. For the more seasoned entomologist, this can develop into an almost obsessive preoccupation.

There is no doubt that butterflies in particular make excellent photographic subjects. The equipment you use, however, can make all the difference between being able to take consistently good photographs or only the occasional lucky one. These days, the only sensible camera to buy as a naturalist is a 35mm SLR. There are a wide range of makes and models on the market with prices to match, from hundreds to thousands of pounds.

Having purchased a camera body, the next most important item of equipment you will need to consider is the lens. You will need one which is specifically designed as a macro (close-focusing) lens or one with a macro facility. There are numerous zoom lenses on the market which offer the latter facility but, on the whole, a fixed focal length macro lens will probably be better in the long run. You may also want to consider buying a tripod, an item of equipment that is really useful when taking close-up shots; a model that is both lightweight and that will allow you to photograph at ground level should be chosen.

Lastly, take great care when choosing your film. Print films have the advantage of providing easily studied photographic records but sooner or later the serious photographer will turn to slide films. Films vary both in terms of quality and colour balance. Although the latter is rather a matter of personal preference, the former can only really be obtained by purchasing film from well-known manufacturers such as Kodak, Fuji or Agfa. All the photographs in this book were taken on film made by one of these three companies.

Butterfly and moth habitats

Butterflies can be found throughout almost the whole of Europe. They occur in nearly every conceivable habitat from the warm, sunny southern regions to high altitudes and the far north where snow and ice dominate for much of the year. This extraordinary geographical and ecological range is a marvel in itself but it also means that the butterfly watcher seldom has far to travel to enjoy seeing these attractive insects.

Dense woodland does not suit most butterfly species, although mature, native forests do support a huge variety of moths. Open, sunny rides are, on the whole, better with clearings and woodland edges providing wonderful hunting grounds for the entomologist. Here may be found the delicate hairstreaks, sometimes accompanied by powerful-flying members of the Nymphalid family, such as White Admirals, fritillaries, Peacocks, Commas, and possibly even that blue-riband butterfly, the Purple Emperor. If uncultivated grassland surrounds the woodland, then the range will include many more species which mingle with the woodland butterflies.

Wild meadows and grazed downland often support a wide variety of butterflies. These include especially the blues, coppers, skippers and browns; the striking Peacock and Small Tortoiseshell will also be found in these grassy areas. If the grassland grades into wetland then a few specialized butterflies (notably the coppers) may abound. However, the fens are perhaps more notable as strongholds for the many moth species that depend on reeds, rushes and other wetland plants for their survival.

Heaths and moorland often have their own characteristic and interesting butterflies. Browns and ringlets frequently predominate and, although their numbers and variety are not so great as in lowland grassland, they are nevertheless well worth studying. Even mountainous regions are well populated with butterflies and moths. The Alps have a particularly well-developed and diverse fauna. The giant Apollo is one of the most spectacular species but there are numerous, specialized high-altitude fritillaries and skippers. Even the extreme north of Scandinavia can boast some unusual polar species.

Gardens, well stocked with flowers, provide wonderful opportunities for watching butterflies and moths. Here, flowers such as Buddleia, Iceplant and Michelmas Daisy provide a magnet for species such as Small Tortoiseshell, Peacock, Red Admiral, whites, Brimstone and Clouded Yellow, the species and flowers to which they are attracted, obviously depending on the time of year. Judicious planting of nectar-rich flowers, together with a tolerance of larval foodplants such as nettles, can make your garden a butterfly haven. After dark, a different set of flowers, such as Tobacco-plant and campions, serve as a source of attraction to the moths.

Swallowtail (British race) *Papilio machaon britannicus*
Wingspan 80 to 90mm

A large and attractive butterfly, impossible to confuse with any other. The upperwings are pale yellow with a network of black vein markings. The wing margins bear blue spots and the hindwings have a conspicuous red spot and tail projection. The underwings show a paler version of the upperwing pattern. In Britain, the Swallowtail is rare and found only in marshes in the Norfolk Broads. The adult is an active insect, on the wing in May and June; sometimes a second brood appears in the summer. Eggs are laid on Milk Parsley and the yellow-green, black and orange larvae feed on the leaves. The pupae overwinters attached to stems of the foodplant.

Swallowtail (European race) *Papilio machaon*
Wingspan 75 to 90mm

A large and showy butterfly. The upperwings are yellow and black, the patterning as for the British Swallowtail. Occurs across most of lowland Europe. It is an insect of waysides and open country, often close to wet ditches. There are two broods in central Europe, flying from May to September; there may be more in southern Europe. The eggs, colourful larvae and pupae occur on Fennel and other members of the Umbelliferae. The SOUTHERN SWALLOWTAIL *P. alexanor* is similar but has bright yellow upperwings with dark transverse bars; it occurs in southern regions of France, Italy and Greece.

14

Scarce Swallowtail *Iphiclides podalirius*
Wingspan 80mm

A large, pale swallowtail, showing the long hindwing tail stream-ers characteristic of the group. The upperwing is very pale yellow with dark bands; the hindwing has a red and blue eyespot and blue markings. The underwings reflect the upperwing patterns. Occurs across most of central and southern Europe. Absent from Britain. It flies at woodland edges and in open country and is an avid nectar feeder, partial to lavender flowers. There are two broods, adults flying in April and May and again in September. The larvae feed on Blackthorn but will also occur on domesticated *Prunus* species.

Southern Festoon *Zerynthia polyxena*
Wingspan 50 to 60mm

A beautiful butterfly. The upperwings bear an intricate pattern with black and red markings on a background of pale yellow. The under-wings show similar patterning but with a paler background colour and more red markings on the forewing. Occurs in south-eastern Europe as far east as Greece. Flies in open country in April and May. Its range is limited by the presence of its larval foodplant, Birthwort, which occurs naturally in scrub and particularly among cultivated vineyards. The larva is curiously fat with red and black-tufted tuber-cles; often found in groups.

15

Spanish Festoon *Zerynthia rumina* Wingspan 45 to 55mm

An attractive butterfly with wing markings resembling the patterns of a stained-glass window. The upperwings have a background colour of rich yellow marked with patterns of black and red. The underwing markings are similar to the upperwing but paler. Occurs in south-east France and the Iberian peninsula. Flies in open country, often being found at altitudes of 1,200m or more, and is on the wing from March to May, depending on altitude. Its range is limited by the presence of its larval foodplant, Birthwort, a species of cultivated and disturbed ground, and woodland edge.

Eastern Festoon *Zerynthia cerisyi* Wingspan 55 to 65mm

A large and showy butterfly. Superficially similar to the Southern Festoon but has fewer dark markings on the wings, these also being less intense. The upperwings and underwings have a background colour of very pale yellow. The Eastern Festoon is an active insect and occurs in south-east Europe from former Yugoslavia and northern Greece eastwards; it also may be found on many Aegean islands and on Crete. It flies in open country and is on the wing from April through to June; it is sometimes seen on lower mountain slopes. Its range is limited by the presence of its larval foodplant, Birthwort, which occurs in scrub and cultivated ground.

False Apollo *Archon apollinus* Wingspan 60 to 65mm

A pale and active butterfly, mature individuals often with rather translucent and waxy-looking wings where the scales have been lost. The upper forewing has smoky-grey and black markings against a whitish background while the upper hindwing has a yellowish background colour with black and red marginal markings. The underwings are similar to the upperwings. Flies during March and April in open country, often in hilly or mountainous districts and, in Europe, is found in Greece. Range linked to the distribution of its larval foodplant, Birthwort.

Apollo *Parnassius apollo* Wingspan 80 to 90mm

A grand and spectacular upland species. Worn specimens often have waxy-looking wings where the scales have been lost. The background colour of the wings is pale creamy white and there are areas of smoky-grey scales and dark spots. There are red eyespots on the hindwings and all the markings are more intense in females than males. Occurs in Alpine meadows in most mainland European mountains including the Alps and the Pyrenees; range extends northwards to Scandinavia. Flies from July to September and is often rather lethargic. Larval foodplants include stonecrops and houseleeks. The SMALL APOLLO *P. phoebus* is similar but the two red hindwing spots are linked by a black bar; occurs only in the Alps.

Clouded Apollo *Parnassius mnemosyne* Wingspan 60mm

A mountain butterfly, somewhat reminiscent of the Black-veined White. The wings are creamy-white and often look rather waxy, especially in worn specimens. The veins are black and there are no red markings on the wings like other apollos. Males have two black marks on the forewing and one on the hindwing; females have two marks on the forewing and variable amounts of grey scaling on the fore- and hindwings. Occurs locally in mountain ranges in eastern Europe from Italy northwards; also found in the Alps, Pyrenees and Massif Central of France. It favours upland meadows and flies from May to July. The larva feeds on *Corydalis*.

Black-veined White *Aporia crataegi* Wingspan 60mm

A distinctive butterfly. The wings may look pure white or rather translucent in some lights due to the sparse scaling. The veins are distinctly defined in black and the markings on the upper-wings and underwings are similar. It is found along hedgerows and at woodland edges. Common across most of Europe, and in some places occurs up to a considerable altitude; in Britain it has been extinct since about 1911. It flies from late June to August and is sometimes seen clustering at wet mud patches in company with skippers and blue butterflies. The larva feeds on Blackthorn and Hawthorn.

Large White *Pieris brassicae* Wingspan 60mm

A familiar and well-known species, often reviled by gardeners. Males have pale upperwings, the forewing with a dark tip and the hindwing unmarked except for a dark mark on the leading edge. Females have two dark spots on the upper forewing and a yellowish hindwing. The underwings of both sexes are similar, the forewing bearing two dark spots and the hindwing being yellowish-green with smoky-grey scaling. Widespread throughout most of Europe. Two or more broods occur and the flight season lasts from April to October. The gregarious larvae feed on nasturtiums and members of the cabbage family. Overwintering pupae are sometimes found on fences and walls.

Small White *Artogeia rapae* Wingspan 50mm

A familiar butterfly and probably Europe's most widespread and common species. The upperwings have an off-white background colour, males having forewings with a greyish tip and single central spot, females with two spots and a dark tip. The hind upperwing in both sexes has a spot on the leading edge. The hind underwing in both sexes is yellowish and the fore underwing has a yellowish tip. Common throughout Europe. Depending on region, there may be two to four broods per year; the flight season is April to October in most parts of Europe, although is more extended in the south. The larva lives singly, feeding on cabbage and related Cruciferae.

Southern Small White *Artogeia mannii* Wingspan 50mm

Very similar to the Small White and best told apart by the more extensive and intense black tip to the upper forewing. The background colour of both upperwings is off-white and males have a single, central, dark spot on the forewing, females having two. The underwings are similar to those of the Small White. Occurs from southern France eastwards at similar latitudes through Europe; it is absent from most of the Iberian peninsula. There may be three or four broods per year, the first one appearing on the wing in March. Larval foodplants include Cruciferae such as Candytuft.

Green-veined White *Artogeia napi* Wingspan 50mm

An attractive butterfly when viewed in close-up and distinctly different from the Small White. The upperwing background colour is white and the veins are outlined with dark scaling. Both sexes have a dark tip to the forewing although this is more pronounced in the female; females have two dark spots on the forewing whereas males have one. The underwings of both sexes are yellowish and the veins are outlined with greenish scales. Common throughout Europe. There are at least two broods and butterflies can be seen on the wing from April to October; woodland rides and waysides are typical haunts for this species whose larvae feed on cresses, Garlic Mustard and other Cruciferae.

Bath White *Pontia daplidice* Wingspan 50mm

A fast-flying, active butterfly. The upperwings are white with variable greyish scaling and dark spots and patches, more pronounced in females than males. The hind underwings are greenish-yellow with white spots and the fore underwings are white with a greenish-yellow tip and two dark spots. Common in southern Europe. It is also a strong migrant species and, on rare occasions, has been recorded as far north as Britain. There are at least two broods in southern regions and butterflies are seen on the wing from March onwards. The larvae feed on the leaves of various Cruciferae.

Peak White *Pontia callidice* Wingspan 35mm

A high altitude butterfly, superficially similar in appearance to the Bath White. The upperwings are white with variable amounts of grey scaling. Males have a prominent black spot on the forewing while females have more extensive black markings. The underside of the forewing is white with a dark spot and yellowish tip; that of the hindwing is yellow, the veins outlined with grey-green scaling. As its name suggests, the Peak White is restricted to mountainous regions, preferring crags and grassy slopes at about 2,000m or more. It is very local, occurring in parts of the Pyrenees, Alps and Dolomites. The butterfly flies in May and June and the larva feeds on Mignonette and mustards.

Dappled White *Euchloe simplonia* Wingspan 35mm

An attractive, active butterfly. The species is rather variable but most have upperwings with a background colour of white. The forewing is tipped with black and bears a black spot; the hindwing has variable patches of grey scaling. The underwings are marbled with greenish-yellow and white patches on the hindwing; the forewing is white with a dark spot and yellowish tip. The Dappled White occurs across most of southern Europe from the Iberian peninsula to Greece. Depending on the region, the flight season extends from April through to June. The larva feeds on members of the Cruciferae family.

Green-striped White *Euchloe belemia* Wingspan 35mm

An active white butterfly with rather pointed forewings. The upperwings have a white background colour; the forewing has a dark spot and a blotched, dark tip while the hindwing has bands of grey scaling. The fore underwings are white with a dark spot and a greenish tip, usually forming distinct bands. The hind underwing has bands of green and white scaling. Occurs in the southern Iberian peninsula, preferring lowland regions. There are two broods per year and the butterfly can be found on the wing from March to May. The larva probably feeds on species of Cruciferae.

Orange Tip *Anthocharis cardamines* 40mm

In many parts of Europe, this butterfly is one of the first signs of spring. Males are extremely distinctive with orange tips to the forewings visible from above and below. The hindwing is dappled with grey scaling on the upper surface and marbled with greenish-yellow below. Females are similar to many species of white. The forewing is tipped with dark grey and there is a dark spot. The underwing is similar to that of the male. Common and widespread in Europe and seen along lanes, hedgerows and woodland edges. They are single-brooded, flying from April to June. The larva feeds mainly on Cuckoo-flower.

Morocco Orange Tip *Anthocharis belia* Wingspan 35mm

An attractive and colourful species. The male has wings with a lemon-yellow background colour and the forewings are tipped with orange. The underside of the hindwing is marbled with dark greenish scaling. The female has wings with a white background colour and a paler orange tip to the forewing than the male. The underside of the hindwing has yellowish scaling and dark greenish marbling. A mainly North African species whose range extends to the Iberian peninsula and parts of southern France. It normally occurs in mountainous regions and has a flight period from May to July.

23

African Migrant *Catopsilia florella* Wingspan 60mm

A strongly migratory African butterfly that has colonized the Canary Islands. At a glance, it could be taken for a Large White but the forewings are more pointed and have a slightly incurved outer margin. The male's upperwings are pale greenish-white with the veins faintly marked with grey; there is a spot in the centre of the forewing. The underwings are more-or-less similar to the upperwings but with a yellow hue. Occurs throughout Africa south of the Sahara and north to Egypt; it also occurs on the Canary Islands. In its normal range, it flies throughout the year, but in the Canaries, it is seen from May to September.

Clouded Yellow *Colias crocea* Wingspan 50mm

An active, fast-flying butterfly and also a strong migrant. The upperwings of both sexes are a rich orange colour with a broad chocolate-brown border. There is a dark, central spot on the forewing and females have yellow spots in the brown border. The underwing is yellow with reddish markings on the hindwing and a few dark spots on the forewing. Originates from North Africa and the Mediterranean but spreads northwards from spring until late summer. In certain years, large numbers reach Britain and northern Europe. It is frequently associated with fields of clover and Lucerne, both of which are foodplants of the larva. The flight season extends from May to October, sometimes longer around the Mediterranean region.

Pale Clouded Yellow *Colias hyale* Wingspan 50mm

An attractive, sun-loving butterfly. The upperwings have a lemon-yellow ground colour although that of the female is much paler than the male. In both sexes, there is a dark central spot on the forewing and both wings have a dark border marked with pale spots. The underwing background colour is yellow, much paler than that of the Clouded Yellow; the underwing markings are similar to this species. Common in central and south-west Europe; a very rare migrant to Britain and northern Europe. This open country species is found particularly in fields of Lucerne, a larval foodplant, and is multi-brooded, flying from May to October.

Berger's Clouded Yellow *Colias australis* Wingspan 50mm

A vigorous butterfly, superficially very similar to the Pale Clouded Yellow. The background colour of the upperwings is brighter yellow, however, and the tip of the forewing is more rounded. The dark border to the upperwings is less extensive than the Pale Clouded Yellow and the central spot on the hindwing is orange rather than pinkish. The underwing colour and markings resemble a very pale Clouded Yellow. Common and widespread in central and southern Europe; a rare vagrant to Britain. The species is multi-brooded, flying from May to October, and is found in open country.

Moorland Clouded Yellow *Colias palaeno* Wingspan 50mm

A distinctive upland butterfly. The upperwings of the male have a lime-green or yellowish background colour with an unmarked dark border and central circle on the forewing. The upperwing colour of the female is almost white. The underwing colour is dull orange although the base of the forewing is pale. This is a butterfly of bogs and moors, occurring in eastern and north-eastern Europe from the Alps northwards through Scandinavia. It flies in June and July and is single-brooded. The larval foodplant is Bog Whortleberry.

Mountain Clouded Yellow *Colias phicomone* Wingspan50mm

An upland, sun-loving butterfly, disappearing the moment the sun goes in. The upperwings of the male are characteristically greenish-grey; those of the female are bright off-white. Both sexes are fringed with delightful pink and the wings bear the patterns typical of all clouded yellows. The underside is lemon-yellow on the hindwings and whitish, tipped with yellow, on the forewing. Local but not uncommon species occurring in the Alps, Pyrenees and Picos de Europa in Spain. It favours flowery slopes and flies from June to August. The larva feeds on Horseshoe-vetch and related plants.

Brimstone *Gonepteryx rhamni* Wingspan 60mm

Usually one of the first spring butterflies, seen as early as February. The wings have a distinctive shape with pointed tips to both the forewing and hindwing. The male is bright yellow and the female is very pale green, almost appearing white; when resting, the butterfly resembles the shape and underside colour of ivy leaves, among which it hibernates. Common throughout Europe, favouring woodland rides and gardens. It is single-brooded, individuals that appear from July onwards hibernating. The larva feeds on Alder Buckthorn, a woodland shrub, and Buckthorn, a chalk downland shrub.

Cleopatra *Gonepteryx cleopatra* Wingspan 60mm

A most attractive butterfly. The shape of the wings is very similar to that of the Brimstone. The male has a background colour of bright yellow but the forewings often have a rich orange central flush. The background colour of the female is pale yellowish-green, almost white. The Cleopatra is a southern European species, restricted to the extreme south of France and regions southwards. It is seen in flowery meadows, woodland and fields of clover and lavender. The butterflies pass the winter as adults, in partial hibernation, and appear again in early spring. The larva feeds on buckthorn.

27

Wood White *Leptidea sinapis* Wingspan 40mm

A delicate butterfly with rather feeble flight. In outline, the wings of both sexes are very rounded and have a ground colour of white. The tips of the forewings are variably tipped with smoky-grey scaling which is more pronounced in males than females. Both sexes are very variable in the depth of yellowish-grey colouring on the underside. The Wood White is a butterfly of woodland rides and adjacent meadows. It is widespread in Europe although its precise distribution is rather patchy; in Britain, it is local or uncommon. There are two broods, the flight season extending from May to August. The larva feeds on various species of vetch and pea.

Eastern Wood White *Leptidea duponcheli* Wingspan 40mm

A delicate, woodland butterfly with a slow and feeble flight. It is rather similar to the Wood White but the wings are usually stained and marked with yellow. The upperwings are yellowish-white and the tip to the forewing is marked with grey, more pronounced in males than females. On the underside, the hindwings are usually distinctly yellow and the whitish forewing is tipped with yellow. The Eastern Wood White occurs locally in southern France and more widely in Greece and Turkey. It occurs in wooded, upland districts and flies in April to May and again in July to August. Larval foodplants include Sainfoin.

Monarch *Danaus plexippus* Wingspan 100mm

World famous as the strongest migrant butterfly. The orange background colour, black veins and the white-spotted black wing margins make this species unmistakable. A North American species which migrates south to Central America in the autumn. A few regularly get caught up in westerly airflows and arrive in western Europe in September and October. The species has also established itself in parts of the Canary Islands and Madeira. All stages in the life-cycle are highly poisonous due to toxins acquired from the larval foodplant, milkweeds. The larva is strikingly marked with black and yellow to deter predators.

African Monarch *Danaus chrysippus* Wingspan 85mm

Also known as the Plain Tiger, this is a large and attractive butterfly. The upperwings are mostly orange with a black margin and extensive black tip bearing white spots. The underwings are more-or-less the same as the upperwings and the sexes are similar. Widespread in Africa, south Asia and Australia; it is resident on the Canary Islands and is a rare vagrant to the eastern Mediterranean. On the Canaries, it is seen visiting flowers in parks and gardens; it flies from May to September. The larva feeds on milkweeds.

29

Nettle-tree Butterfly *Libythea celtis* Wingspan 45mm

A distinctive butterfly with an unusual wing shape and characteristic markings. The forewings are dark brown but with several orange-buff patches; their margin is jagged and uneven. The hindwings are dark brown with a large orange-buff patch and scalloped-edged margins. The underside of the forewings resembles the upper surface; the underside of the hindwing is uniform grey-brown. Occurs across the warmer regions of southern and south-east Europe eastwards into Asia. It favours wooded regions where the foodplant of the larva, Nettle-tree, grows. The butterfly flies in July and August, then hibernates and appears in the following spring.

Two-tailed Pasha *Charaxes jasius* Wingspan 75 to 80mm

A magnificent butterfly with a powerful flight. The outline of the wings superficially resembles that of the Purple Emperor but this species has two characteristic tail streamers on each hindwing. The upperwings are rich brown with a creamy margin bordered with black. The underwings are beautifully marbled with chestnut, purple-grey, white and cream. The Two-tailed Pasha is the single European representative of a genus whose stronghold is North Africa. It lives along the south coasts of Spain, France, Italy and westwards to Greece. There are two broods, in May–June and in August–September. The larval foodplant is the Strawberry-tree.

Purple Emperor *Apatura iris* Wingspan 60 to 65mm

One of Europe's most impressive butterflies, although rather elusive. The upperwings of both sexes have a brown background colour with a series of white patches forming a band on the hindwing. The sexes differ in the male having a purple iridescence to the wings which is usually visible only on one pair of wings at a time. The underwings of both sexes are chestnut and dark brown with white patches reflecting the upperwing pattern. Occurs in northern and central Europe, including southern Britain. It is a woodland butterfly on the wing in July and August, found almost exclusively in ancient oak woods with mature Common Sallows, the larval foodplant.

Lesser Purple Emperor *Apatura ilia* Wingspan 55 to 60mm

An elusive, woodland butterfly. It is rather similar to the Purple Emperor but smaller and more marked with grey and black. The upperwings of both sexes have a dark brown ground colour with characteristic white bands and one orange-ringed dark spot per wing; the male's upperwings have a purple iridescence and the female is often yellowish. Occurs in central and southern Europe, excluding Britain. It flies in woodland and is also seen flying low along valleys. There are sometimes two broods, the first in May–June, the second often in August–September. Larval food-plants include willows and poplars, especially Aspen.

White Admiral *Limenitis camilla* Wingspan 50mm

An attractively marked butterfly with a powerful, gliding flight. The upperwings are sooty black in both sexes with white patches forming a more-or-less complete band on the fore- and hindwings. The underwings have a rich chestnut background colour with black and white spots and white patches that reflect the upperwing pattern. It is a woodland butterfly that occurs across central Europe including the south of Britain. It is single-brooded, flying from June to August. The larval foodplant is Honeysuckle and the adults are fond of visiting and feeding on the flowers of Bramble.

Southern White Admiral *Limenitis reducta* Wingspan 50mm

An attractive butterfly with a powerful flight. In appearance it is superficially similar to the White Admiral but, on the upperwings, the background colour is usually blacker and the white markings are broader. On the underwings, the background colour is usually brick red rather than orange. The wings are more rounded than the White Admiral. Occurs in central and southern Europe but not in Britain. It is a woodland species, favouring sunny rides and woodland edges, and is on the wing from May to July. The larval foodplant is Honeysuckle.

Hungarian Glider *Neptis rivularis* Wingspan 50mm

Superficially similar to the White Admiral but with narrower and much more rounded wings. Its flight is particularly charming and distinctive with little flits and then long glides that characterize the genus. The upperwings are very dark brown with a broken band of white on each wing. The underside is orange-brown with white markings similar to those on the upperwings. Found in Austria and central east Europe. It is local but not rare and flies in open woodland in May and June, and then again from July to September. The larva feeds on Goat's-beard Spiraea.

Camberwell Beauty *Nymphalis antiopa*
Wingspan 80mm

A large and showy species. The wing shape is distinctive with a characteristic jagged margin. The upperwings are a rich maroon, bordered with blue spots and fringed with a creamy margin. The underwings are smoky brown with a white margin; sexes are similar. Widespread in Europe but a very rare migrant to Britain, having first been found at Camberwell in London; in America it is known as the Mourning Cloak. It occurs in open woodland and scrub. The adult is on the wing from June to August and, after hibernation, in March and April. Larval foodplants include willow, sallow, birch and elm.

Large Tortoiseshell *Nymphalis polychloros* Wingspan 80mm

A fast-flying, attractive butterfly. The wings have typically jagged margins. The upperwings are orange-brown with black and yellow patches and a dark margin. The underwings are smoky brown; the sexes are similar. Widespread in Europe, though very rare in Britain. There is one brood; the butterflies emerge in June or July, hibernate without feeding and appear again in April to feed on liquids and bask in the sun. It is an insect of woodland edge, fields and hedgerows. The larvae are gregarious until pupation and feed on elm, although they will take willow, poplar, cherry and other trees.

Yellow-legged Tortoiseshell *Nymphalis xanthomelas* Wingspan 80mm

An attractive but rather local butterfly. It is fairly similar to the Large Tortoiseshell and best distinguished by its yellow-brown middle and hind legs. The upperwings are orange-brown with similar markings to the Large Tortoiseshell; the black border that defines the blue spots on the hindwing is, however, broader and more diffuse. The underwings are smoky brown and the sexes are similar. Found in Austria and central east Europe, occurring in woodland, and flies from July to September. The gregarious larvae construct silken nests in willow trees.

Peacock *Inachis io* Wingspan 60mm

A colourful and well-known butterfly. The wing margins have a typically ragged outline. The upperwings are maroon with a single startling yellow, maroon and blue eyespot on each of the forewings and a blue and buff eyespot on each of the hindwings. The underwings are smoky brown. Widespread in Europe, including Britain. Common in open fields, downs, woodlands and gardens, and wherever flowers grow; it is particularly fond of Buddleia and thistles. The insect is single-brooded; it flies from July to September and again, after hibernation, from early March to May. The sole larval foodplant is Common Nettle and the larvae live communally within a web of silk.

Red Admiral *Vanessa atalanta* Wingspan 60mm

An active and familiar butterfly. The upperwings have a black background colour with bands of red on the forewings and hindwings and white spots on the former. The hind underwing is attractively marbled with black, brown and blue, and the fore underwing has markings that reflect the upperwing pattern. Found throughout Europe including Britain. It is a strong migrant, spreading northwards from the Mediterranean region each summer to breed. It is multi-brooded; adults hibernate and a few survive the winter in Britain. The solitary larvae feed on Common Nettle. In autumn, adults feed on rotting fruit.

Painted Lady *Vanessa cardui* Wingspan 60mm

An attractive butterfly of open places. The upperwings have a salmon-pink background colour with patterns of black with white spots. The underwings are marbled with buff, white and brown; the forewings are tinged with pinkish-buff. Occurs throughout Europe. It prefers fields and downs, but sometimes visits garden flowers; it is a fast flier, particularly when disturbed, but often returns to the original spot. Painted Ladies are continuously brooded but survive the winter only in the extreme south. The flight season lasts from April to October and individuals seen in Britain are invariably migrants. The larval foodplants include thistles and burdocks.

Small Tortoiseshell *Aglais urticae* Wingspan 42mm

One of the most attractive and familiar European butterflies. The upperwings have an orange background colour and are marked with yellow, brown, black and blue. The underwings are coloured with smoky brown and yellowish-buff. Occurs throughout Europe and is one of the commonest British butterflies, especially from July to September. There are two to three broods, flying from early March to October and hibernating as adults, sometimes in groups. It is attracted to flowery places, especially gardens. The gregarious larvae live in a silken web and feed mainly on Common Nettle.

Comma *Polygonia c-album* Wingspan 45mm

A beautiful butterfly with ragged-edged wing margins that look almost tattered. The upperwings are orange-brown with black and pale orange spots; the first generation adults have paler wings with more yellow-orange markings. The underwings are smoky brown and the hindwings bear a conspicuous 'comma' mark that gives the species its name. It is found throughout Europe including Britain, and is generally common except in the north. This species prefers hedgerows, woodland edges and gardens. There are two broods, the flight season extending from March through to September; adult butterflies hibernate. The larva, which resembles a bird dropping, feeds on Common Nettle, but can also be found on Hop and elm.

Southern Comma *Polygonia egea* Wingspan 45mm

An attractive, southern European butterfly. It is rather similar to the Comma but the orange-brown upperwings have far fewer black markings, especially on the hindwing. The underside is marbled with grey and smoky brown; the 'comma' mark on the hindwing is reduced to a small 'y' mark. Found locally in north-central Spain and southern France, and more widely from Italy eastwards. It favours dry, sunny habitats and often bare slopes with rocky outcrops where the larval foodplant, Pellitory-of-the-wall, flourishes. The adult flies in May and June and again in August and September; the second brood hibernates and flies again in early spring.

Map Butterfly *Araschnia levana* Wingspan 42mm

Best known for its intricate and delicate wing patterns. There are two broods each year, the first generation resembling a fritillary with orange-brown wings marked with dark brown and streaked with white. The second generation resembles a miniature White Admiral, the dark brown wings having white markings. The underwings of both generations resemble a map, with blue, reddish-brown and buffish-yellow markings. Common in central Europe but absent from Britain. It flies from April to September and frequents rough ground and wooded areas. The larva feeds on Common Nettle.

Silver-washed Fritillary *Argynnis paphia* Wingspan 60mm

An attractive butterfly with a powerful, gliding flight. The upperwings are orange-brown and marked with dark spots and lines; the upperwings of the female are often more greenish-buff. The underwings are greenish and buffish-orange with metallic, shiny patterns on the hindwing. The forewings are rather pointed compared to other fritillaries. A woodland butterfly which is common all over Europe, although, in Britain, it is found only in the south. It flies from June to August and has a single brood. The larvae, which hibernate, feed on violet leaves.

Cardinal *Pandoriana pandora* Wingspan 70mm

The largest European fritillary and powerful in flight. The upper-wings are pale orange-buff with an attractive greenish suffusion and black spots and lines. The underside colouring is bright pink and green with dark spots on the forewing; the female has silver stripes on the hindwing. A southern European species found in Spain, southern and western France, Italy and eastwards to Greece. It frequents flowery meadows and woodland edges. It loves thistle flowers and lime blossom and flies from June to August. The larva hibernates as soon as it hatches and feeds on violets the following spring.

Dark Green Fritillary *Mesoacidalia aglaia* Wingspan 60mm

A powerful flier and well able to withstand the strong winds in the exposed locations it inhabits; if blown off course, it swings round and continues flying on course with ease. The upper-wings are orange-buff with black spots and stripes. The underside has greenish scaling and silvery spots on the hindwing and orange-buff forewings with dark and silver spots. It occurs throughout most of Europe, where it is locally common; in Britain, it is seldom numerous. Its preferred habitats include downland, meadows and coastal dunes. It flies during July and August and the larvae feed on violets.

High Brown Fritillary *Fabriciana adippe* Wingspan 60mm

An attractive butterfly, powerful in flight. The upperwings are rich orange-brown with dark spots and markings on both wings. The underside has greenish scaling and silver spots on the hindwing, the forewing being orange-brown with dark spots. The silver spots are absent in form *cleodoxa*. Occurs across central and southern Europe where it is not uncommon in suitable habitats; in Britain, however, it is endangered. It frequents flowery meadows, woodland edges and uplands and appears on the wing in July and August, being single-brooded. The larvae feed on Dog Violet leaves.

Queen of Spain Fritillary *Issoria lathonia* Wingspan 42mm

An active, fast-flying butterfly. The margins of the wings have rather straight edges and sharp angles compared to most other fritillaries. The upperwings are orange-brown with dark spots. The underside is orange-buff, the hindwings having large, silvery spots and the forewings black spots. Not uncommon in southern and eastern Europe where it flies in flowery grassland and at the edges of woodland. It is also a strong migrant and on rare occasions even reaches Britain. There are two or more broods, depending on the location, and the species flies from February to October. The larval foodplants are violets.

Shepherd's Fritillary *Boloria pales* Wingspan 35mm

An upland species, sometimes encountered in small groups well above the snow line. The wing shape and markings on the upper-wings are distinctly angular in comparison with other *Boloria* species. The upperwings are orange-brown while the underside is buffish-brown with white spots on the hindwing. Occurs on mountain slopes in mainland Europe over 1,500m. Its distribution is patchy, the species occurring in the Pyrenees, Alps, Balkans, Poland, the Czech Republic, Germany and Spain. There is one brood, butterflies being on the wing from June to August. The larvae feed on violets.

Mountain Fritillary *Boloria napaea* Wingspan 40mm

As its name suggests, a mountain butterfly usually found around the tree-line. The upperwings are orange-brown with variable black markings. The underside ground colour is buffish-brown; there are brown, black and white markings on the hindwing but the markings on the forewing are usually very faint. Occurs very locally in the Pyrenees, but more widely in the Alps and northern Scandinavia. It favours wet Alpine meadows where the larval food-plant, Alpine Bistort, grows. The butterfly is on the wing in July and August.

Marbled Fritillary *Brenthis daphne* Wingspan 40mm

A bright, attractive species that has noticeably round wings. The upperwings are orange-buff and marked with dark spots. The underside is orange-buff and has yellow and whitish marbling on the hindwing and black spots on the forewing. The Marbled Fritillary flies in sunny valleys and hills with abundant flowers in southern and central Europe, where it is locally common; it is absent from Britain, western parts of Spain and Portugal. There is one brood each year and the flight season extends from June to August. The larva hibernates; larval foodplants include violets and bramble.

Small Pearl-bordered Fritillary *Clossiana selene* Wingspan 40mm

A small and attractive fritillary with swift flapping flight, often gliding low over the ground. This species can be confused with the similar Pearl-bordered Fritillary and is best distinguished by studying the underside of the hindwing. The Small Pearl-bordered has several silver spots in addition to the border of seven pearls whilst the Pearl-bordered has only two. The upperwings are orange-brown with dark spots. Occurs in northern and central Europe including Britain; it is absent from southern Spain, southern France and Italy. It flies in June and July and prefers open woodland.

Titania's Fritillary *Clossiana titania* Wingspan 50mm

An attractive upland and northern butterfly. The wings are rather broad and rounded and the orange-brown upperwings have particularly bold and angular black markings. The underside has a characteristic pinkish-purple hue with sharp markings; the purple coloration is stronger in the Alpine race. Found in parts of the Pyrenees, most of the Alps and part of the Baltic region. Its range also extends from the extreme east and south of Scandinavia and central Europe eastwards to Russia. It favours light woodland and adjacent meadows and flies from June to August. Larval food-plants include violets and Bistort.

Pearl-bordered Fritillary *Clossiana euphrosyne* Wingspan 42mm

A beautifully marked woodland butterfly. The upperwings are orange brown and marked with black spots and lines; the precise markings are rather variable. The underside is orange-buff with dark spots on the forewing and the hindwings with seven silvery pearls on the borders and two silver spots. Found throughout Europe except southern Spain; it is locally common. Forest rides in deciduous woodland is a favourite habitat. One brood is usual, flying in May and June but in hot summers, a second brood may occur in August. The larval foodplant is Dog Violet.

Violet (Weaver's) Fritillary *Clossiana dia*
Wingspan 35mm

A relatively small, delicate butterfly sometimes occurring in rather hilly regions. The upperwings are rich orange-brown with extensive black markings and spots. The underside shows mottled violet-brown and white markings on the hindwings and orange-buff forewings with black spots. Occurs across central Europe from France to northern Greece but is absent from Britain. There are two or three broods per year, the flight season lasting from May until August. Preferred habitats include open woodlands and heaths and larval foodplants include violets and bramble.

Thor's Fritillary *Clossiana thore* Wingspan 45mm

A northern and upland fritillary. The upperwing colour varies according to race from dark orange-brown to buffish-brown; variable amounts of dark markings also occur. The underside is reddish- to orange-brown with dark markings on both wings and yellowish markings forming a crescent. Occurs in the Alps and in northern Scandinavia. It is on the wing in late June and July and is usually only found above an altitude of 1,000m in the Alps. The butterfly often occurs along woodland edges and the larvae feed on violets.

44

Glanville Fritillary *Melitaea cinxia* Wingspan 40mm

A sun-loving butterfly with attractively marked upper and lower wings. The upperwing colour is orange-buff with a network of dark markings. The underside is pale with orange-buff patterning and black spots. The five round black spots on the underside submarginal band are diagnostic. Widespread and fairly common in southern and central Europe. It is absent from southern Spain and in Britain occurs only on the Isle of Wight. It flies on flowery slopes and in most of Europe there are two broods flying in May and June, and again in August and September. The gregarious larvae feed on plantains.

Knapweed Fritillary *Melitaea phoebe* Wingspan 50mm

A variable species, sometimes rather similar to the Glanville Fritillary. The upperwing colour is usually orange-buff and the species can be distinguished best by the large orange submarginal crescent in the third space of the forewings. On the hindwings, black spots in the underside orange submarginal band are usually absent. Widespread and common in southern and central Europe; it is absent from southern Spain and Britain. It favours flowery fields and hillsides and, at low levels, there are two broods from April to August. Larval foodplants include knapweeds and plantains.

Spotted Fritillary *Melitaea didyma* Wingspan 35 to 50mm

A distinctive, upland butterfly. The male is most easily recognized with its deep orange upperwings and relatively few dark spots. The female's upperwings are a more drab buffish-orange. The undersides show orange and buff bands on the hindwings and orange forewings with small, dark spots. Common and widespread through much of central and southern Europe to 1,800m; it is absent from Britain and northern France. It flies on mountain slopes and flowery meadows from May to August. Larval foodplants include plantains, toadflaxes and speedwells.

False Heath Fritillary *Melitaea diamina* Wingspan 40 to 48mm

An unusually dark fritillary. The upperside is very dark brown, especially the hindwings although there are small orange spots. On the underside of the hindwing, there are small, round spots between the white crescent and orange submarginal band. Widespread in southern and central Europe; it is not found in Britain, southern and central Spain or southern Greece. It is generally single-brooded and flies in June and July. Shady grassland is preferred, especially if scattered trees are present. The gregarious larvae feed on plantains and cow-wheats.

Heath Fritillary *Mellicta athalia* Wingspan 44 to 48mm

A sun-loving, woodland fritillary. The upperwings are orange-brown with a network of dark markings. The underwings are marked with orange, buff and white. The lack of dark spots in the submarginal band of crescents on the underside hindwing distinguishes it from other small fritillaries. Widely distributed in Europe; absent from southern Spain and, in Britain, is endangered with small colonies in southern England. One to three broods occur from May to September and it invariably occurs in colonies. The gregarious larvae feed mainly on Common Cow-wheat but will also take Woodsage and plantains.

Meadow Fritillary *Mellicta parthenoides* Wingspan 40mm

An attractive but rather variable fritillary. The upperwings are orange-brown with thin, black markings; females usually have paler, buffish submarginal bands. The underside is buffish-brown with creamy spots forming a band. Best distinguished by a black discal spot lying obliquely on the underside forewing. Widespread in Spain, Portugal, France, south-west Bavaria and south-west Switzerland. It prefers damp meadows, especially on lower mountain slopes. Usually two broods, flight seasons being May and June, and August and September. Larval foodplants include cow-wheats and plantains.

Nickerl's Fritillary *Mellicta aurelia*
Wingspan 35mm

A small fritillary which is often found at considerable altitudes. The upperwings are orange-brown with broad, dark markings. The underside is orange-brown with marginal pale spots on the hindwing and a submarginal pale band. Nickerl's Fritillary is fairly widespread in central Europe in a band from central France eastwards. It favours flowery meadows and pastures, often up to altitudes of 1,200m or more. There is usually a single brood with butterflies on the wing in July and August. Larval foodplants include plantains, cow-wheats and speedwells.

Provençal Fritillary *Mellicta deione* Wingspan 40mm

An attractive butterfly which is superficially similar to the Heath Fritillary. The best distinguishing feature is the absence of the five black spots in the submarginal orange band seen on the underside of the hindwing. The upperwings are orange-brown with a network of dark markings. As its name suggests, it is found in the Provence region of southern France. Its range also extends to the Iberian peninsula but it is absent from the interior and north of this region. It favours flowery meadows and often occurs on the lower slopes of mountains. Larval foodplants include toadflaxes.

Cynthia's Fritillary *Hypodryas cynthia*
Wingspan 42 to 50mm

A sun-loving Alpine butterfly. The male is instantly recognisable by its unique white patterning on the upperwing which contrasts with the orange and black markings more typical of other fritillaries. The female is larger, without white, and has a soft orange ground colour with a low contrasting pattern. The underside resembles that of the Marsh Fritillary but the ground colour is more yellowish-orange. Flies on mountain heaths with Juniper and Blueberry. Scarce and restricted to the Alps and an area in Bulgaria, usually above 2,000m; flies in July. Larval foodplants include lady's mantles and plantains.

Marsh Fritillary *Eurodryas aurinia* Wingspan 40 to 52mm

A slow-flying species which is only active during sunny periods. The upperwings have a beautiful patterning of orange, dark brown and yellow. The underwings are orange-brown with paler patches and spots. Widespread throughout Europe except northern Scandinavia. It is becoming endangered in Europe and is possibly commonest in Britain; even here it is, however, still very local. Despite its name, this species is not confined to marshes, and also occurs on chalk grassland and on high ground. The single brood flies from May to July. The gregarious larvae feed on Devil's-bit Scabious and plantains.

49

Spanish Fritillary *Eurodryas desfontainii*
Wingspan 45 to 50mm

An attractive butterfly associated with sunny mountain slopes in Spain. The species superficially resembles the Marsh Fritillary but the background colour of the upperwings is brick red not orange-brown; there are conspicuous black spots on the upper hindwing. The underwings are orange brown and have the paler markings clearly defined by dark lines and borders. Confined to southern and eastern parts of Spain and the eastern Pyrenees. It frequents Mediterranean scrub at altitudes up to 1,200m and is on the wing in May and June. Larval foodplants include scabiouses.

Marbled White *Melanargia galathea*
Wingspan 50mm

A distinctive, colonial butterfly. The upperwings are subject to considerable variation but are a marbled mixture of black and white patches; the ground colour also varies. The underside patterning is a reflection of that of the upperside with the black replaced by yellowish-grey and the white by cream. It is found across much of Europe except Scandinavia; in Britain, it occurs in the south of England. Favours grassland and is often locally abundant, attracted to flowers of knapweeds, thistles and scabiouses. It flies from June to September and the larva feeds on grasses.

Spanish Marbled White *Melanargia ines*
Wingspan 50mm

An attractive, upland butterfly. It is superficially similar in appearance to the Marbled White, having upperwings patterned with a mixture of black and white patches. Similarly, the underside pattern is a reflection of that on the upperwings although considerably less intense. One reasonably reliable feature, however, is the presence of a wide, black bar across the cell on the forewing, visible from above and below. Occurs throughout most of the Iberian peninsula except the north. It lives in meadows at around 1,500m and flies in May and June. The larva feeds on grasses.

Western Marbled White *Melanargia occitanica*
Wingspan 55mm

An attractive species, usually associated with upland regions. The wing patterns are superficially similar to the Marbled White but a close examination usually reveals a black bar across the cell of the forewing; on the underside this is usually incomplete. The veins on the underwing usually appear outlined in brown scaling and the eyespots on the hindwing are conspicuous. Occurs in the southern and central Iberian peninsula and the far south of France. It occurs at altitudes of up to 1,500m and favours grassy hillsides. It is on the wing from May to July and the larva feeds on grasses.

51

Esper's Marbled White *Melanargia russiae* Wingspan 50mm

An attractive, southern European butterfly. Like other marbled white species, the upperwings have a well-defined patchwork of black and white markings; on the forewing there is a thin, and often incomplete line crossing the cell and on the hindwing, a noticeable round white patch near the base of the wing. The underside markings resemble those of the upperwings although areas of black are often replaced by grey scaling or are absent. Occurs in central and eastern Spain and locally in the south of France, Italy and the Balkans. Favours grassy meadows at altitudes of 1,000m or more and flies in June and July. The larva feeds on grasses.

Common Grayling *Hipparchia semele* Wingspan 50mm

A sun-loving butterfly of warm, dry places. The upperwings are brown with a band of yellow-buff containing two eyespots on the forewing and one on the hindwing. The underside shows a camouflaged pattern of grey and brown on the hindwing and orange and yellow-buff on the forewing with two eyespots. At rest, the hindwings often conceal the forewings; the butterfly characteristically adopts an angle to the sun that casts the least shadow. Occurs across most of Europe including Britain; it is absent from a few Mediterranean islands. It favours stony and rocky places, cliffs and heaths and flies from June to August. The larva feeds on grasses.

Woodland Grayling *Hipparchia fagi* Wingspan 70mm

An active, alert butterfly. The upperwings are dark, blackish-brown with a broad, submarginal whitish band on both wings. The pale band contains two eyespots on the forewing and one on the hindwing; it is broader on the hindwing in the female than in the male. The underside has a similar pattern to the upperside with the lower wing pattern diffused by greyish scaling. Widespread in Europe from northern France eastwards to Greece; it is absent from Britain, Scandinavia and most of Spain. As its name suggests, it is a woodland species which flies in July and August. The larva feeds on grasses.

Rock Grayling *Hipparchia alcyone* Wingspan 60mm

An upland and mountain butterfly that can tolerate dry seasons better than other species. The upperwings are dark brown with a band of creamy-yellow on each wing; there is one large eyespot on the forewing and one small spot on each of the wings. The underside shows grey, brown and white patterning on the hindwing, the pattern on the forewing being similar to that on its upper surface. The Rock Grayling occurs throughout Iberia, the south of France, Austria and the Czech Republic. It is a butterfly of mountain slopes and dried-up river beds and flies in June and July. The larva feeds on grasses.

Southern Grayling *Hipparchia aristaeus* Wingspan 65mm

A widespread and rather variable butterfly. Females in particular can look very similar to the Common Grayling with upperwings that are brown with buffish-yellow submarginal bands and two eyespots on the forewing, one on the hindwing. The male usually has upperwings with broader, more orange submarginal bands. The underside has marbled grey and brown on the hindwing and forewings that recall the pattern on their upper surface. Has a very restricted distribution in Europe, occurring in Corsica, Sardinia, southern Greece and Turkey. It favours hot, stony places and flies in June and July.

Striped Grayling *Pseudotergumia fidia* Wingspan 60mm

A butterfly of warm regions with attractively marked underwings. The upperwings are more-or-less uniformly dark brown with two eyespots on the forewing, a dark submarginal line on both wings and variable amounts of white, mostly on the forewings. The underside is beautifully patterned on the hindwing with black, white and brown; the forewing has two, yellow-ringed black eyespots. Occurs in the south of France and throughout Iberia except the north-west. It favours rocky, grassy slopes and flies in July and August. The larva feeds on grasses.

Alpine Grayling *Oeneis glacialis* Wingspan 50mm

A high altitude butterfly with a restricted distribution. The upper-wings are characteristically buffish-orange; both sexes have small eyespots on both wings but the female's are more pronounced. The underside shows fine markings of grey and brown on the hindwing and a buffish-orange forewing bearing an eyespot. Occurs at around 1,800m in the French and Italian Alps and just into Austria. It favours rocky, grassy slopes and flies, briefly, in June and July. The larva feeds on grasses, hibernating amongst the roots, covered with snow for much of its life.

The Hermit *Chazara briseis* Wingspan 50 to 60mm

A subtly marked and attractive species which varies in size considerably. The upperwings are dark brown with clear white bands which are broken on the forewing and contain two eyespots on each wing. The underside is patterned with brown, grey and buffish-white and there are two eyespots on each forewing. Mainly a southern European butterfly but its range extends north to Brittany; it is absent from Britain and western Iberia. It favours dry, rocky places, even up to 2,000m, and is on the wing in June and July. The larva feeds on grasses.

Great Sooty Satyr *Satyrus ferula* Wingspan 55 to 65mm

An upland species of brown butterfly. The upperwings are dark sooty brown with a faint paler band on the hindwing, and an orange submarginal band on the forewing contains two large and conspicuous eyespots and one smaller one between them. The underside shows grey, buff and pale brown patterning on the hindwing and an orange-buff forewing with two large, dark eyespots. A southern European species occurring from southern France eastwards to Greece; it is absent from the Iberian peninsula. It favours rocky slopes and flies in July and August. The larva eats grasses.

Black Satyr *Satyrus actaea* Wingspan 55 to 65mm

A rather sombrely coloured butterfly. The upperwings are uniformly very dark brown with a hint of a paler band, especially in females; the forewings have two eyespots in the female and one in the male. The underside is marbled grey, brown and black with two black and two white diffuse submarginal bands on the hindwings and one of each on the hindwings; there are two eyespots on female forewings and one on male forewings. Occurs in southern and central Iberia and southern France. It prefers rocky slopes from 1,000 to 2,000m and flies in July and August. The larva feeds on grasses.

The Dryad *Minois dryas* Wingspan 50 to 60mm

Notable for its large, rounded wings and dark colouring. The upper-wings are rich brown in colour with two, blue-centred black eye-spots on the forewing and one on the hindwing. The larger female is much less dark than the male and her eyespots are usually larger and more prominent. The underside is similar to the upperside but usually with a paler background colour etched with dark scaling. Range is a band across central Europe, excluding most of Spain and Italy; it is absent from Britain and Scandinavia. It occurs in open country and grassland from sea level to 1,000m or more. The flight season lasts from June to August and the larva feeds on grasses.

Tree Grayling *Neohipparchia statilinus* Wingspan 50mm

Recalls a rather drab version of a Grayling. The upperwings are uniformly dark brown with a hint of paler submarginal banding, more noticeable in females than males; there are usually two faint dark eyespots on the forewings and two tiny white spots. The underwings are a mixture of grey, brown and pinkish-buff with two dark eyespots on the forewing. Occurs across much of Europe but is absent from Britain and Scandinavia. It prefers rocky places with trees, in which it often rests. It is on the wing from July to September and the larva feeds on grasses.

False Grayling *Arethusana arethusa* Wingspan 40 to 50mm

An active, fast-flying butterfly. The upperwings are pale brown with yellow-buff bands containing two dark spots on the forewing and one on the hindwing; the coloration of males is more intense than females. The underside shows marbled grey, brown and buff on the hindwing and a yellowish forewing with one small eyespot. Occurs locally across much of central Europe from northern France southwards to Spain and eastwards to Austria and the Czech Republic; it is absent from Portugal and most of Italy. It favours wild, open grassland and flies in July and August. The larva feeds on grasses.

Great Banded Grayling *Brintesia circe* Wingspan 60 to 70mm

One of the largest Satyrids and a truly striking butterfly. The upperwing markings recall those of the White Admiral: they are mostly black with a clear, white band on both wings. The underside, however, is completely different and clearly that of a grayling, with bands of grey, brown, black and white, and an eyespot on the forewing. Occurs from southern Europe up to the north of France and eastwards to Greece and beyond. It is found in fields, woodland edges and open country and is on the wing from June to August. The larva feeds on grasses.

Small Mountain Ringlet *Erebia epiphron* Wingspan 32mm

A high altitude butterfly which is only active during periods of sunshine. The upperwings are a rich, dark brown with a band of orange-red containing four or five dark spots on the rather angled forewing and three or four on the hindwing. The underside is superficially similar to the upperside although the orange-red band is less distinct. Occurs in scattered upland locations from northern Spain, across France and the Alps eastwards; in Britain, it occurs in the Lake District and in Scotland. It favours craggy slopes and flies in July and August. The larva feeds on grasses.

Scotch Argus *Erebia aethiops* Wingspan 40mm

An attractive, upland butterfly. The upperwings are dark sooty brown with well-defined brick-red bands containing three or more eyespots on the forewing and three or more on the hindwings. The underside is paler brown with buffish bands and dark eyespots on the forewing. Found locally from central France, through the Jura and Alps to Greece and beyond; it is absent from Spain and the Pyrenees. In Britain, it occurs locally in northern England and more widely in Scotland. The butterfly favours high ground and flies from July to September. The larva feeds on grasses.

59

Yellow-spotted Ringlet *Erebia manto* Wingspan 40mm

An Alpine butterfly with distinctive markings on its underside. The upperwings are dark brown with orange-brown bands containing small, black spots. The underside shows a dark hindwing bearing conspicuous yellow markings; the forewing pattern resembles that on its upper surface. Its main distribution is in the eastern Alps but it also occurs locally in the Pyrenees and Tatra Mountains. It is found in Alpine meadows at around 1,500m or more and flies during July and August. The larva feeds on grasses.

Swiss Brassy Ringlet *Erebia tyndarus* Wingspan 35mm

An Alpine butterfly with a very restricted distribution. The upperwings have a ground colour of dark brown but a metallic, brassy sheen; there is an orange band on the forewing containing two small eyespots but the hindwing is unmarked. The underside has marbled grey, brown and black on the hindwing and the forewing is orange and grey-tipped with two small eyespots. Confined to the central Alps. It favours mountain grassland at around 2,000m and flies in July and August. The larva feeds on grasses. The COMMON BRASSY RINGLET *E. cassioides* is similar but with larger eyespots; it occurs in many southern European mountains.

Almond-eyed Ringlet *Erebia alberganus* Wingspan 40mm

An Alpine butterfly with distinctive markings on the wings. The wings have a dark brown ground colour on both surfaces. The orange bands on the wings are broken into pupilled ovals; these are visible on both the upperside and underside of the wings. It should be noted, however, that this species, and indeed all the Erebias, are subject to considerable variation. Limited to small areas of northern Spain, the southern French Alps, Switzerland, northern Italy and the Apennines. It flies in Alpine meadows at altitudes of 1,200 to 1,800m and is on the wing in June and July. The larva feeds on grasses.

Sooty Ringlet *Erebia pluto* Wingspan 50mm

An extremely variable Alpine butterfly. In some races, the wings can be almost black on both upper and lower surfaces, with small eyespots occasionally visible. In other races, the ground colour is sooty brown with orange bands or larger areas of orange appearing on the forewings or on both wings; eyespots may be present or absent. It has a limited range, occurring in the Alps and the Apennines. It favours stony, grassy slopes at altitudes between 2,000m and 3,000m and is one of the few species to live this high. It flies in July and August and the larva feeds on grasses.

Dewy Ringlet *Erebia pandrose* Wingspan 50mm

An upland and northern species with distinctive markings. The upperwing ground colour is dark brown; the forewings show a broad area of orange, cut by a dark transverse line, the outer segment containing four small, black spots in a row; the hindwings have three, orange-ringed dark spots. The underside is marbled grey and brown on the hindwing with two dark, transverse lines; the orange forewing shows four small, black dots in a row. Occurs in the eastern Pyrenees, Alps, Tatra Mountains and in northern Scandinavia. It favours grassy places at around 2,000m in the south but at lower elevations in the north and flies in June and July.

Marbled Ringlet *Erebia montana* Wingspan 50mm

A slow-flying, upland butterfly. The upperwings are rich, dark brown with orange-red bands containing eyespots; there are two large and usually one or two smaller spots on the forewing and three or four on the hindwing. The underside shows marbled grey, brown and white on the hindwing with a jagged, narrow white band; the forewing is orange-brown with pupilled eyespots. Occurs in the Alps and locally in the Apennines at altitudes around 2,000m. It favours rocky and grassy slopes and flies in July and August. The larva feeds on grasses.

Large Ringlet *Erebia euryale* Wingspan 40mm

An attractive, upland butterfly. Superficially similar to the Scotch Argus but with the fringed margins to the wings chequered and not uniform. The upperwings are dark brown with orange-red bands containing three or more dark spots on each wing. The undersides are paler, smoky brown, the orange-red bands containing pupilled eyespots. Occurs in mountain regions (1,000 to 2,000m) from northern Spain, across central and southern France, through the Alps to Greece. It occurs in light conifer woodland, among the grasses, foodplants for the larva. It flies from July to September.

Piedmont Ringlet *Erebia meolans* Wingspan 50mm

A sun-loving, high altitude species which resembles the Scotch Argus. The upperwings are dark brown with orange bands containing pupilled, dark eyespots; the number of spots and intensity of the bands is variable. The underside is dark brown, the hindwing having a pale marginal band with pupilled, dark eyespots and the forewing having an orange band with pupilled, dark eyespots. Occurs in northern and central Spain, the Pyrenees, much of the Alps up to southern Germany and into Austria. It occurs in high Alpine meadows up to 2,000m and flies in June and July. The larva feeds on grasses.

Arran Brown *Erebia ligea* Wingspan 50mm

An attractive, upland butterfly. The upperwings are a rich, dark brown with orange bands containing white-pupilled dark eyespots. The underside is also dark brown and shows an orange band with eyespots on the forewing; the hindwing has orange-fringed spots and a diagnostic white band. Occurs in southern Sweden and from the Alps and Jura Mountains eastwards at altitudes up to 1,500m. It reputedly once occurred on the Isle of Arran but is not now found in Britain. It flies in grassland, usually amongst conifers, in July. The larva feeds on grasses.

Woodland Ringlet *Erebia medusa* Wingspan 40mm

A sun-loving butterfly of grassy places. The upperwings are dark brown with orange-yellow bands on the forewings containing two large, and one or more smaller, eyespots; on the hindwing, the dark spots are ringed with orange-yellow. The underwings resemble the upperwings. All the markings are, however, somewhat variable. Less of a high altitude butterfly than many other *Erebia* species. It occurs from central France eastwards and is absent from Britain. Meadows and grassy woodland rides are favoured, the butterfly flying in May and June. The larva feeds on grasses.

Water Ringlet *Erebia pronoe* Wingspan 45mm

A slow-flying woodland butterfly. The upperwings are dark brown with bright reddish-orange bands. On the forewing, these contain twinned eyespots and a third slightly smaller eyespot, usually with a tiny spot between them. On the hindwing, the band contains three spots. On the underside, the forewing pattern recalls that on the upper surface; the hindwing is marbled with bluish-grey and brown. An upland woodland species, occurring in the Alps, locally in the Pyrenees, and in the Tatra Mountains. It is seen in grassy clearings and flies in August and September. The larva feeds on grasses.

Ringlet *Aphantopus hyperantus* Wingspan 48mm

A familiar butterfly of grassy places. The upperwings are dark, almost black in males but sooty brown in females; two dark spots, sometimes white-pupilled, are seen on fore- and hindwings. The underside is also dark brown but the dark eyespots are clearly ringed with white. Occurs across most of Europe including Britain but is absent from south-west Iberia, southern France, Italy and northern Scandinavia. It favours meadows and grassy woodland rides and is really a lowland butterfly but occurs up to 1,500m in places. It flies in June and July and the larva feeds on grasses.

Giant Grayling *Berberia abdelkader* Wingspan 80mm

A large butterfly with noticeably rounded wings. The upperwings are mostly dark brown; the hindwing is paler towards the margin and shows two dark spots while the forewing is very pale, almost white towards the margin and tip, with two dark eyespots. The underwing pattern reflects that on the upper surfaces but the veins on the hindwing are pale. Essentially a North African species but might occur as a vagrant to southern Iberia. It often favours the fields of Lucerne and flies from May to August as two broods.

Meadow Brown *Maniola jurtina* Wingspan 50mm

Probably Europe's commonest butterfly, sometimes occurring in dense colonies. The upperwings are sooty brown; on the forewing, males have a small orange patch containing an eyespot while, in females, the orange forms a larger band containing one large eyespot. The underside shows a brown hindwing with a paler band and orange and buff forewings with an eyespot. The extent of the markings in both sexes is variable. Occurs across most of Europe including Britain. It favours grassy places from lowlands up to 1,500m or so and flies from June to September. The larva feeds on grasses.

Gatekeeper *Pyronia tithonus* Wingspan 40mm

A very common and well-known summer butterfly. The upperwings are orange-brown bordered with dark brown; there is a dark, twin-pupilled spot on the forewing. The underside is mottled grey and brown on the hindwing with a rich chestnut band; the forewing pattern resembles that of its upper surface. Occurs throughout Europe except northern Britain and Scandinavia. It is a butterfly of meadows, downs, hedgerows and lanes and does not occur at high altitudes. It flies in July and August and often clusters together to feed on marjoram, ragwort and other flowers. The larva feeds on grasses.

Spanish Gatekeeper *Pyronia bathseba* Wingspan 35 to 50mm

An attractive little butterfly of early summer. The upperwings are orange-buff with dark brown borders; there is a large, dark, twin-pupilled eyespot on the forewing and usually four smaller dark spots on the hindwing. The underwings have a broad, cream band on the hindwing (a good identification feature) and white-ringed dark spots; the forewing markings recall the upperwing pattern. Occurs in Spain and southern France. It favours sparse woodland, among conifers and on dry, rocky ground, usually at low altitudes. It flies from April to July and the larva feeds on grasses.

67

Southern Gatekeeper *Pyronia cecilia* Wingspan 35mm

An attractive butterfly, usually common within its range. The upperwings are orange-brown and show a broad border of darker brown; the forewings have an oval, twin-pupilled eyespot. The underside is marbled grey and brown on the hindwing; the forewing patterns and colours are similar to those on its upper surface. Occurs in Spain, along the south coast of France to Italy and beyond. It prefers sunny, Mediterranean habitats, sometimes at considerable altitudes, and flies from May to August in two broods. The larva feeds on grasses.

Large Heath *Coenonympha tullia* Wingspan 38mm

A sun-loving butterfly, usually associated with moors and upland places. The upperwings are buffish-orange; males usually have a more intense colour and small spots on the wings. The underwings are grey-brown on the hindwing with a jagged, creamy band and white-ringed, dark eyespots; the forewing is orange-brown, bordered with grey and with small spots. Occurs from northern Europe, including northern Britain, southwards to central France, the Alps and eastwards. It is rather local and flies in June and July. The larva feeds on grasses.

Small Heath *Coenonympha pamphilus* Wingspan 30mm

A very common grassland butterfly. The upperwings are orange-brown, bordered with dark brown; there is a dark spot on the forewing. The underside shows chestnut-brown scaling on the inner hindwing, the grey outer margin separated by creamy scales; there are red-ringed spots on the hindwing. The forewing pattern recalls that of the upper surface. Occurs throughout Europe. It is on the wing from May to September in a succession of broods, but from the end of May onwards in Britain and the north. It favours grassy waysides and meadows and the larva feeds on grasses.

Corsican Heath *Coenonympha corinna* Wingspan 30mm

A small, active, grassland butterfly. The upperwings are orange-brown, bordered with dark brown, the forewing band broader towards the tip; single eyespot on the forewing. The underside shows an orange-brown forewing with an eyespot; the hindwing is reddish-brown and grey, the colours separated by a jagged, creamy line; the intensity of the spots on the hindwing varies according to location. Found on Corsica, Sardinia and Elba; very local on mainland Italy. Occurs in grassy places, usually around 1,000m, and flies from June to August. The larva probably feeds on grasses.

69

Pearly Heath *Coenonympha arcania* Wingspan 35mm

An attractively marked grassland butterfly. The upperside shows orange-brown forewings, bordered with dark brown; the hindwing is dull brown with a paler band and bordered with dark brown. The underside shows orange-brown forewings with a single spot; the hindwing is dark brown with a broad, submarginal white band and conspicuous pearly eyespots. Widely distributed in Europe but absent from Britain, much of Spain and Scandinavia. It occurs in grassland and slopes up to 1,800m, flying in June and July. The larva feeds on grasses.

Darwin's Heath *Coenonympha darwiniana* Wingspan 32mm

Formerly considered to be a race of Pearly Heath that was more-or-less confined to higher elevations in the Alps. The upperside shows orange-brown forewings, broadly bordered with dark brown, the same colour as the uniform hindwings. The underside shows orange-brown forewings and darker hindwings bearing a row of yellow-ringed eyespots, the row backed by a pale stripe. Occurs in the Alps and very locally elsewhere. It favours meadows at altitudes of 1,500m or more and flies in July and August. The larva feeds on grasses.

Alpine Heath *Coenonympha gardetta* Wingspan 35mm

As its name suggests, a high altitude butterfly with attractively marked underwings. The upperwings are buffish brown, suffused with olive brown towards the margins, with forewing eyespots usually reduced or absent. The underside hindwing has a characteristic and diagnostic broad, white band with eyespots that are not ringed. Has a restricted range from the French Alps through Switzerland to Austria and Italy. It flies in Alpine meadows at altitudes of around 2,000m and is on the wing in July and August. The larva feeds on grasses.

Dusky Heath *Coenonympha dorus* Wingspan 34mm

An active little butterfly of warmer climates. The upperwings are orange-brown but are suffused to a greater or lesser degree with dusky scaling; there is an eyespot on the forewing and small spots on the hindwing. The underside shows orange-brown on the forewing with a prominent eyespot; the hindwings have a broad, jagged-edged transverse stripe and several submarginal small eyespots. Main range is in Iberia south of the Pyrenees; it also occurs in the south of France and very locally in central Italy. It favours sunny, stony slopes and flies in June and July. The larva probably feeds on grasses.

Chestnut Heath *Coenonympha glycerion*
Wingspan 35mm

A richly coloured butterfly. The upperwing is chestnut-brown, sometimes with small spots showing on the hindwing but otherwise unmarked. The underside shows a sooty brown hindwing with conspicuous white-pupilled eyespots and a pale, jagged line; the upperwing is orange-brown with a small eyespot. Mainly an eastern European species whose range extends westwards to Germany and northern Italy; it also occurs locally in western France. It is a grassland species which occurs in hilly regions to altitudes of 1,500m and flies in June and July. The larva feeds on grasses.

Speckled Wood *Pararge aegeria tircis* Wingspan 45mm

A common butterfly of wooded places. Across most of its range, the upperwings are dark brown with pale cream markings, a single eyespot on the forewing and three spots on the hindwing. The underside shows light and dark brown marbling on the hindwing while the forewing pattern reflects that on its upper surface. Occurs throughout Europe including Britain but, in Scandinavia, it only occurs in the south. In southern Europe, this race is replaced by the southern form (see next description). It favours sunny woodland rides and glades, and grassy places, flying from April to October in successive broods. The larva feeds on grasses.

Speckled Wood, southern form *Pararge aegeria aegeria*
Wingspan 45mm

The southern European form of the familiar Speckled Wood from northern and central Europe. The deep orange ground colour on both surfaces of the wings is often so intense that specimens could be mistaken for the Wall Brown at a glance. There is a single eyespot on the forewing and three spots on the hindwing. The underside shows light and dark brown marbling on the hindwing while the forewing pattern reflects that on its upper surface. This distinctive race occurs from Iberia, through southern France to Italy and beyond. It favours shady wooded areas and flies from April to October in successive broods. The larva feeds on grasses.

Wall Brown *Lasiommata megera* Wingspan 45mm

A common and attractive butterfly that could potentially be confused with a fritillary. The upperwings are orange-buff marked with dark lines; there is a single eyespot on the forewing and two or more on the hindwing. The underwing shows a camouflaged marbling of grey and brown on the hindwing with small eyespots; the forewing pattern recalls that on its upper surface. Occurs throughout most of Europe except northern Britain and most of Scandinavia. It favours dry, rocky grassland with bare soil patches. This habitat preference and its habit of accompanying a walker are clues to its identity. It flies from May to September and the larva feeds on grasses.

73

Large Wall Brown *Lasiommata maera*
Wingspan 45 to 50mm

A sun-loving butterfly with beautifully marked underwings. The upperwings are grey-brown in males but richer brown in females; males have a large, twin-pupilled eyespot plus a tiny satellite spot on the forewing, the hindwing having three small spots; females have similar spots lying on orange-yellow bands. The underside shows mottled grey and brown on the hindwing with several small eyespots; the forewings are grey and reddish with a conspicuous yellow-ringed, dark eyespot. Occurs throughout most of Europe except Britain. It flies from June to August and the larva feeds on grasses.

Woodland Brown *Lopinga achine* Wingspan 50mm

A distinctive and easily recognized butterfly. The wings are sooty brown above and below and both surfaces have rows of large, yellow-ringed dark eyespots which are much larger than on the Ringlet. On the underwings, the spots are bordered by an irregular pale line. Females are similar to males but may have rather larger eyespots and more rounded wings. Local, but widely scattered across central Europe; it is absent from Britain, Scandinavia and most of Spain. As its name suggests it is a woodland species which flies in June. The larva feeds on grasses.

Duke of Burgundy Fritillary *Hamearis lucina*
Wingspan 30mm

Despite its name, not related to true fritillaries. The upperwings are a chequered mixture of rich brown and orange, females usually being brighter than males. The underside is orange-buff with spots and patches of black and white. Occurs across much of Europe as far north as southern Scandinavia including southern England; absent from most of Spain, Holland and north Germany. Its presence in fields and woodlands depends on the presence of its larval foodplants, Primrose and Cowslip. It flies from May to July; in the south there may be more than one brood and an extended flying season.

Brown Hairstreak *Thecla betulae* Wingspan 40 to 50mm

An often sluggish butterfly of scrubby areas. The upperwings of the male are uniform brown except for orange at the base of the tail streamer and hindwing apex; the female has a conspicuous orange patch on the forewing. The underside of both sexes is orange-brown with black and white lines on both wings. Occurs across most of Europe including southern England; it is scarce and patchy in Spain and absent from Scandinavia except the southern tip. It favours Blackthorn hedges and light, wooded scrub, flying in July and August. The larval foodplant is Blackthorn.

75

Purple Hairstreak *Quercusia quercus* Wingspan 38mm

A butterfly that is invariably associated with mature trees in oak woodlands and seldom strays far from the canopy. The upperside of the male is dark iridescent purple all over; the female has a bright purple forewing patch. The underside of both sexes is lilac-grey with black and white lines on both wings and a small orange spot near to the tail streamer. It can be found throughout Europe wherever oak trees are dominant; the range includes Britain and southern Scandinavia. The entire life-cycle takes place on the oak tree, the buds of which are food for the larva.

White-letter Hairstreak *Strymonidia w-album* Wingspan 35mm

An intriguingly named and local butterfly. The upperwings are uniformly dark brown in both sexes. The underside is rich brown with a row of orange, submarginal crescents on the hindwing; there is a white line or streak on both wings, on the hindwing forming the letter 'w'. Occurs across much of Europe including Britain. It favours hedgerows and woodlands, its precise distribution being dictated by the presence of its larval foodplant trees, English Elm and Wych Elm. The butterflies live in colonies, fly in July and seldom stray far from their host tree except perhaps to feed on Bramble flowers.

Black Hairstreak *Strymonidia pruni* Wingspan 35mm

An often lethargic butterfly that frequently crawls among the foliage. The upperwings are brown with a broken submarginal band of orange on the hindwing; on the forewings, this is more extensive in females. The underside is brown with a submarginal orange band on each wing, black dots and white lines or streaks. Occurs widely in central Europe; in Britain, it is rare and restricted to a few woods in Buckinghamshire and Oxfordshire. It is found in open woodland in the vicinity of the larval foodplant, Blackthorn. Adults fly in July and are fond of visiting the flowers of Privet and Bramble.

Blue-spot Hairstreak *Strymonidia spini* Wingspan 35mm

A local and perhaps declining species. Males have upperwings which are uniformly brown except for two orange spots on the hindwing; females have broad bands of orange on their brown upperwings. The underside of both sexes is grey-brown with a smoothly curving white streak on each wing and a prominent blue hindwing spot near the tail streamer. Local but widespread in Europe; it is absent from Britain and the northern countries. It is found in rough scrub and open woodland where the larval foodplants, Blackthorn and Buckthorn, grow, and it flies in June and July.

Green Hairstreak *Callophrys rubi* Wingspan 25mm

An active, well camouflaged butterfly. The upperwings are uniform brown and the underwings are green, with a slight sheen and a faint, broken white line on the hindwing. Found throughout Europe, including Britain, and is local but occasionally common. It occurs at the edges of woodland and amongst bushes, scrub and hedgerows, sometimes up to 1,800m. It flies as early as March in southern Europe but elsewhere is seen in May and June. The larval foodplants for this species are extremely varied and include, among others, gorse, rock-rose, dogwood, heathers and trefoils.

Provence Hairstreak *Tomares ballus* Wingspan 25mm

A not very appropriately named butterfly, resembling a cross between a Small Copper and a Green Hairstreak. The upperside shows orange forewings broadly bordered and faintly spotted with brown; the hindwings are brown with an orange margin. The underside shows a green hindwing bordered with brown and orange forewing with dark spots and a brown border. Despite its name, it has its stronghold in central and southern Spain though it does occur on the adjacent Mediterranean coast of France. It favours rough ground and flies from January to April. The larva feeds on Bird's-foot Trefoil.

False Ilex Hairstreak *Nordmannia esculi* Wingspan 35mm

A rather drab little hairstreak. The upperwings are a uniform dark brown; females have two orange spots at the rear angle of the hind-wings while males only have one. The underside is grey-brown with a broken white streak on the hindwing with small, submar-ginal orange spots more pronounced in males than females. Restricted to Spain, the Pyrenees and the extreme south-west of France; it is local throughout its range. It is found in areas of rough scrubby ground with smaller oak trees (the larval foodplant) and flies in June and July.

Ilex Hairstreak *Nordmannia ilicis* Wingspan 35mm

A common but rather nondescript hairstreak. The upperwings are brown with an orange patch on the forewings, more pronounced in females than males; there is also an orange spot on the rear angle of the hindwing. The underside is grey-brown, darker in males than females; there is a broken white streak on both wings and orange submarginal marks on the hindwings. Widespread across most of Europe but absent from Britain and almost all of Scandinavia; it is commonest in the south. It favours rough, open land with oaks and oak scrub (the larval foodplant) and flies in June and July.

Small Copper *Lycaena phlaeas* Wingspan 30 to 38mm

An active and beautifully marked little butterfly. The upperside is rather variably marked with orange and dark brown: the forewings are mainly orange with dark spots and a dark border while the hindwings are brown with an orange submarginal band. On the underside, the patterning is similar to the upperside but with the dark brown replaced by grey-brown. Occurs throughout Europe, including Britain. It favours flowery meadows, waste ground and even gardens and flies from April to October in two broods or more. The larva feeds on docks and sorrels.

Large Copper *Lycaena dispar* Wingspan 35 to 50mm

An attractive wetland butterfly. The male has orange upperwings with a dark border. The female's upperwings are orange-yellow with a dark border, dark spots on the forewing and dark-streaked hindwings. The undersides show an orange-buff forewing with a grey margin and a grey hindwing with an orange border; both wings are suffused with black spots. Occurs locally across central Europe. The Dutch race *L. dispar batavus* has been established at Woodwalton Fen Reserve in Cambridgeshire. It favours water meadows where the larval foodplants, Great Water Dock and other docks, grow. The race *batavus* flies in July but race *L. dispar rutilus* has two broods, flying from May to September.

Scarce Copper *Heodes virgaureae* Wingspan 28 to 40mm

A beautiful grassland butterfly. The male has pure orange upper-wings with a dark border; those of the female are orange-brown, suffused with dark spots. The underside is orange-buff, both wings marked with a few, dark spots and the hindwings with larger white spots, but there is considerable variation across its range. Occurs from north and central Spain and the Pyrenees eastwards into most of Europe; it is absent from northern France, the Benelux Countries and Britain. It favours grassy meadows, often in mountains, and flies in July and August. The larva feeds on sorrels and docks.

Sooty Copper *Heodes tityrus* Wingspan 30 to 35mm

A rather sombre-looking copper. The upperwings are brown, suffused with dark spots and with orange spots on the margin; the male's wings are dark brown while those of the female are brighter, almost orange-brown. The underside is grey-brown, with both wings dotted with dark spots and with a border of orange spots. Has a wide distribution and occurs across most of Europe except southern Iberia, Britain and most of Scandinavia. It favours open country and flowery meadows and flies in two broods in April to May and August to September. The larva feeds on sorrels and docks.

81

Purple-shot Copper *Heodes alciphron* Wingspan 40mm

An active and sun-loving butterfly. The upper-wings of the female are dark brown with an orange border to the hindwing; those of males from northerly races have a strong, iridescent purple flush to the otherwise brown wings. The southern race has an orange ground colour in both sexes, the male with a slight purple flush. The underside of both sexes is grey-brown with both wings suffused with dark spots and the hindwings with a border of orange spots. Occurs in most of Europe except Britain, Scandinavia and the north-west. Lives in flowery meadows; flies in June and July. The larva feeds on sorrels and docks.

Purple-edged Copper *Palaeochrysophanus hippothoe*
Wingspan 32 to 40mm

A most attractive butterfly when the upperwings are seen. Males have dark-bordered orange upperwings with broad, purple streaks on the hindwing. The female is very variable but typically has dull orange forewings with dark spots and brown hindwings with an orange border. The underside of both sexes is grey-brown with dark spots; the forewings often have an orange hue and there is an orange border to the hindwing. Widespread in Europe but absent from southern Spain, west and north France and Britain. It favours flowery meadows and flies in June and July. The larva feeds on bistorts and docks.

82

Grecian Copper *Heodes ottomanus* Wingspan 30mm

An active little copper. The upperwings are pure orange with a few small dark marks on the forewing and a dark border on both; the hindwing dark border is rather indented. The underside is typical of many other copper butterflies: the forewing is orange and studded with black spots; the hindwing is grey-buff with an orange sub-marginal band and dark spots. As its name suggests, found locally in Greece, especially in the vicinity of Athens; it is widespread in Turkey. It favours warm, flowery places and flies in two broods, the first in April and May and the second in August and September. The larva feeds on docks.

Long-tailed Blue *Lampides boeticus* Wingspan 35mm

A vigorous, fast-flying butterfly with a tail-streamer on the hindwing. The male's upperwings are lilac-blue with a dark margin to the forewing and a dark spot near the tail streamer; those of the female show more brown, the blue being confined to a broad patch on the forewing. The underside is grey-buff marked with concentric but irregular bands on pinkish-buff, darker than the ground colour. A strong migrant whose natural home is southern Europe. Not uncommon from the Alps southwards; very rarely even reaches Britain. It favours flowery meadows and flies from May to October in continuous broods. The larva feeds on members of the pea family.

Short-tailed Blue *Everes argiades*
Wingspan 30mm

A small but active butterfly which is a surprisingly strong migrant. The hindwings bear a short tail streamer. The male has violet-blue upperwings with a dark margin while the female's are dark brown. The underwing is pale grey and suffused with small dark spots and small orange spots on the hindwing margin. Occurs from northern Spain to Brittany and eastwards to Russia. It is commonest in the south and is an extremely rare migrant to Britain. Flowery meadows are the preferred habitat and the butterfly has two broods, flying throughout the summer months.

Provençal Short-tailed Blue *Everes alcetas* Wingspan 32mm

An active butterfly, rather similar to the Short-tailed Blue. The male's upperwings are pale violet-blue with a very narrow dark margin; those of the female are dark brown, sometimes almost black. The undersides are pale grey with small, black spots. Occurs locally in southern Europe especially southern France and central Spain. It favours flowery meadows, especially where members of the pea family and in particular Crown Vetch (a favourite larval foodplant) grow. It flies from April to September in two or more broods and is often quite common.

Lang's Short-tailed Blue *Syntarucus pirithous*
Wingspan 25mm

An attractive butterfly with short tail streamers. The male upperwings are lilac-blue with a hint of dark barring; the female is more heavily patterned with brown. On the underside, grey-buff concentric bars mark the ground colour of off-white and there are two bluish spots near the tail streamer. Ranges from Spain to Greece along the entire south coast of Europe. Migration to the north coast of Europe occurs each summer, stopping short of Britain. Seen on dry hillsides and is continuously brooded, flying from March to October. The larva feeds on brooms, Lucerne and related plants.

Small Blue *Cupido minimus* Wingspan 25mm

A small butterfly, very active in sunny weather. The upperwings of both sexes are a similar charcoal colour but the male has a dusting of gunmetal-blue scales, particularly in the basal areas. The underside of both sexes is pale blue-grey with a few, small, white-bordered black spots and blue scaling near the wing base. Occurs throughout Europe including Britain, but is absent from southern Spain and northern Scandinavia. It favours flowery grassland, usually on chalk or limestone, where the larval foodplant, Kidney-vetch, flourishes. There is a single brood with butterflies on the wing in June and July.

Lorquin's Blue *Cupido lorquinii* Wingspan 25mm

An attractive butterfly, rather similar to the Small Blue; the ranges of the two species, however, do not overlap. The upperwings of the male are deep violet-blue with a dark border; those of the female are charcoal colour, sometimes with blue scaling towards the basal areas. The underside of both sexes is pale blue-grey with a few, small, white-bordered black spots and blue scaling near the base. Restricted in Europe, occurring only in southern Spain and locally in south-west Portugal. It favours areas of short, flowery grassland, sometimes up to 1,500m, and has a single brood flying in May and June.

Holly Blue *Celastrina argiolus* Wingspan 30mm

An attractive butterfly seen both in spring and autumn. The upper-wings are chalky blue; males have unmarked wings while females have a black margin and apex which is stronger in the second generation. The underside of both sexes is pale bluish-white with a scattering of small, black dots. Range extends across Europe except the north of Scotland and north Norway. It favours woodland rides, inland cliffs and even gardens, indeed anywhere where Holly and Ivy grow in close proximity. First brood eggs are laid on Holly and second brood on Ivy, but also Buckthorn and other shrubs.

Iolas Blue *Iolana iolas* Wingspan 40mm

A showy blue with a distinctly southern distribution. The upper-wings of the male are a deep violet-blue with black margins; those of the female are a similar colour but the margins are much wider and more extensive. The undersides of both sexes are grey-brown with a row of dark spots on each wing. Occurs in southern Europe from southern France to Greece; there are isolated populations in south-east Spain. It favours sunny, open woodland and maquis habitat from low levels up to 1,500m and flies in May and June. The larva feeds on Bladder Senna.

Silver-studded Blue *Plebejus argus* Wingspan 24 to 30mm

A delightful little butterfly, fond of sunning itself. The upperwings of the male are deep violet-blue with a dark margin and white border; those of the female are brown (rare aberrant forms can be blue) with a border of orange spots and crescents. The underside of both sexes is grey-brown with rows of black spots and an orange marginal band, most prominent on the hindwing, where it highlights blue spots. Occurs across most of Europe except for Scotland and northern Norway. In Britain, it is essentially a heathland species but elsewhere it occurs on grassy slopes. The flight season is roughly May to August and larval foodplants include Ling and gorses.

87

Zephyr Blue *Plebejus pylaon* Wingspan 30 to 35mm

A sun-loving butterfly, often found in mountain regions. Its appearance is variable, the species occurring as several races. Male upperwings vary from blue to violet-blue and have dark veins, a dark margin, sometimes with faint orange spots around the border. Females usually have brown wings with orange, submarginal spots. The underwings are grey-brown with dark spots and an orange submarginal band. Occurs locally in Greece, the Alps and central Spain. It favours sunny, grassy slopes up to 1,500m and flies in May and June. The larval foodplants include species of vetches.

Idas Blue *Lycaeides idas* Wingspan 30mm

A widespread and often common butterfly that is confusingly similar to the Silver-studded Blue at first glance. The upperwings of the male are purplish-blue with a dark margin and veins marked darker towards the margin. Females have brown upperwings, usually with little or no blue suffusion, and orange submarginal spots reduced or absent. Occurs throughout most of Europe although it is absent from southern and western Iberia and Britain. Preferred habitats range from grassland to upland slopes depending on where it occurs and it flies in June and July. The larva feeds on various vetches and related plants.

Cranberry Blue *Vacciniina optilete* Wingspan 25mm

A northern and upland species of blue. The upperwings of the male are pure, deep violet-blue; those of the female are a rich, dark brown. The undersides are grey-brown with rows of bold, black spots and one or more orange spots on the margin of the hindwing. Range includes all of Scandinavia and south into central Europe as far as the Alps. It is a butterfly of moorland and bogs, or scrubby woodland at high altitudes in Alpine regions; it is invariably associated with the larval foodplant, Cranberry. The single brood is on the wing in July.

Brown Argus *Aricia agestis* Wingspan 25mm

An attractive butterfly, sometimes mistaken for a female Common Blue or other species. The upperwings are a rich, dark brown and the submarginal band of prominent orange crescent marks, particularly strong in Spanish specimens, helps in identification. The underwings are grey-brown with rows of black spots and a submarginal band of orange spots. The sexes are similar although females have more rounded wings and often bolder markings. Occurs throughout Europe except northern Britain and northern Scandinavia; it is usually rather local. It favours grassy slopes and flies from May to August. Larval foodplants include rock-roses and cranesbills.

Northern Brown Argus *Aricia artaxerxes* Wingspan 25mm

Similar to Brown Argus but ranges usually not overlapping. The upperwings are a rich, dark brown with a submarginal band of orange spots; in Britain, the species is distinguished from the Brown Argus by the white discoidal spot on the forewing. The underwings are usually brown with white-ringed black spots and an orange submarginal band on both wings; in continental Europe, this band is absent from the forewing. Occurs in northern England and Scotland, throughout Scandinavia, and locally in the Alps and northern and central Spain. It favours upland, usually calcareous, grassland and flies in June and July. The larva feeds mainly on rock-roses.

Geranium Argus *Eumedonia eumedon* Wingspan 30mm

A northern or upland blue. The sexes are similar, the upperwings being unmarked and dark brown, sometimes appearing nearly black. The underside is brown with black spots and an orange submarginal hindwing band typical of many blues; there is usually a pale wedge on the hindwing. Occurs in central and eastern Europe and Scandinavia; fragmented colonies are also found in the Alps, Italy, south-west France and northern Spain. It is a grassland species, occurring either at low levels or in mountains according to area and latitude. The single brood flies in July and the larva feeds on species of cranesbills.

Escher's Blue *Agrodiaetus escheri* Wingspan 35 to 40mm

Rather similar to the Common Blue but usually larger and brighter. The upperwings of the male are blue with a violet tinge towards the base; those of the female are rich brown with a sub-marginal band of orange crescentic spots. The underwings of both sexes are greyish with a row of white-ringed dark spots and sub-marginal orange spots; there is no spot in the forewing cell. Found in eastern Spain, southern France, Italy and on the Baltic coast. It prefers hilly grassland and long grass meadows, and flies in June and July. The larva feeds on milk-vetches and Sainfoin.

Amanda's Blue *Agrodiaetus amanda* Wingspan 40mm

An attractive sun-loving butterfly. The male has pale blue upper-wings with a dark margin, widest on the forewing; those of the female are brown and show orange and black submarginal spots on the hindwing. The underside is pale brown with rows of black spots and orange submarginal spots typical of many blues. Has several strongholds in eastern Spain and its range spreads east-wards along the French coast to the Alps where it broadens north-wards into Sweden; it is absent from Britain and western France. It favours grassy banks and meadows and flies in June and July. The larva feeds on Tufted Vetch and Sainfoin.

91

Chapman's Blue *Agrodiaetus thersites* Wingspan 32mm

An active little southern European butterfly. Both sexes are very similar in appearance to the Common Blue and are only safely distinguished by the absence of this latter species' underside spot in the forewing cell. Males have violet-blue upperwings and are noticeably hairy; the upperwings of females are rich brown with a submarginal band of orange crescentic spots. The underside shows a grey-brown ground colour, a submarginal band of orange crescentic spots and dark rows of spots on the wings. Widespread in southern Europe, its northern limits being the northern Alps and the Jura. It favours grassy areas where its larval foodplant, Sainfoin, grows, and flies from May to July in two or more broods.

Meleager's Blue *Meleageria daphnis* Wingspan 40mm

An attractive butterfly, recognized by the colour and shape of the wings. The hindwings in both sexes have scalloped margins, the feature enhanced in the female by wing markings. Both sexes have sky-blue upperwings but the female's forewings have a dark fore-edge band and broad dark margins; the hindwing also has dark margins. The underside is pale grey in the male and pale brown in the female; there are dark spots on the wings but only faint markings on the margins. Its range is from north-east Spain through southern France and Italy into central Europe and Greece. It favours grassy hillsides and flies in June and July. The larva feeds on legumes and Thyme.

Chalk-hill Blue *Lysandra coridon* Wingspan 40mm

A characteristic chalk downland butterfly. The male has chalky-blue upperwings with dark margins; females have brown wings and small, submarginal orange spots on the hindwing. The undersides are grey with blue scaling towards the wing bases; there are rows of black dots on the wings and submarginal orange spots on the hindwing. The species shows considerable variation. Occurs across most of Europe including southern Britain; it is absent from Scandinavia. Its preferred habitats occur almost exclusively on chalk and limestone where short turf is interspersed with flowers. It flies in July and August and the larva feeds on Horseshoe-vetch.

male (above) female (below)

Provence Chalk-hill Blue *Lysandra hispana* Wingspan 40mm

Very similar in appearance to the Chalk-hill Blue and perhaps best distinguished in the field by flight season. The male has chalky-blue upperwings with dark margins; females have brown wings and a submarginal band of orange spots on both wings. The underside is grey-brown with prominent dark spots and orange submarginal spots similar to the Chalk-hill Blue. Occurs mainly in Provence, France, the range just extending into Spain to the west and Italy to the east. It favours grassy places and flies in two broods, the first in April and May, and the second in September (Chalk-hill Blues fly between these two broods).

Adonis Blue *Lysandra bellargus* Wingspan 32mm

One of the most attractive European blues. Male upperwings are vivid iridescent blue, brighter than most other species; the black-spotted fringes distinguish it from the Common Blue. Females usually have brown upperwings but often show varying amounts of blue. The underwings are grey-brown with white-ringed black spots and submarginal orange spots, most noticeably on the hindwings. Widespread in Europe but local and becoming rarer in Britain. It favours chalk grassland and has two broods, flying in May to June and July to August. The larva feeds on Horseshoe-vetch.

Spotted Adonis Blue *Lysandra punctifera* Wingspan 34mm

A mainly North African species, rather similar in appearance to the Adonis Blue. Males have upperwings that are deep iridescent blue; the wing fringes are black-spotted and there are submarginal black spots on the hindwing. Female upperwings are usually brown with variable amounts of blue scaling. The underside is grey-brown with heavy, black spots and submarginal orange spots. Occurs in Morocco and might occasionally be seen as a vagrant in southern Spain. It favours grassy places, often at considerable altitude and flies in May to June and again in August to September.

Mazarine Blue *Cyaniris semiargus* Wingspan 30mm

A small and attractive butterfly. The upperwings of males are violet-blue while those of females are dark brown, sometimes appearing almost black. The undersides are uniform brownish with a simple arrangement of small, white-ringed black spots and bluish scaling towards the base. Now extinct in Britain; elsewhere in Europe it is ubiquitous and often common in suitable habitats. It prefers flowery meadows with long grass and flies in June and July. The larva feeds on trefoils, Sainfoin and related members of the pea family.

Damon Blue *Agrodiaetus damon* Wingspan 33mm

A mainly mountain species of blue. The male has sky-blue upperwings with broad dark margins and dark veins radiating in from the margin; female upperwings are uniform dark brown. Both sexes have undersides that are brown with a comet-like oblique streak across the hindwing, in addition to a small number of dark spots on both wings. Occurs in northern Spain and the Pyrenees, the Alps and eastwards into central Europe. It favours upland hay meadows with long grass and flies in July and August. The larva feeds on Sainfoin.

95

Furry Blue *Agrodiaetus dolus* Wingspan 35mm

A very local blue from southern Europe. The upperwings of the males resemble a rather grubby Chalk-hill Blue, the sky-blue being suffused with varying amounts of brown; the wing margins are dark. Females have brown wings with a submarginal band of orange spots. The body and wing bases of both sexes are silky-hairy. The underside is grey-brown with unmarked margins but dots on the wing surfaces. Occurs locally in southern France and central Italy. It favours upland meadows and flies in July and August. Larval foodplants include Lucerne and Sainfoin.

Turquoise Blue *Plebicula dorylas* Wingspan 32mm

A mountain species of blue butterfly. The male has deep turquoise blue upperwings, similar in colour to Amanda's Blue. The female has brown upperwings with a few orange submarginal crescentic spots on the hindwing. The underside is grey-brown with white margins containing dark spots between the veins; there is a pale wedge on the hindwing. Occurs from northern Spain, where it is local, through southern France and Italy into Greece and central Europe. It occurs on grassy slopes at elevations of 1,000 to 2,000m and flies from May to July. The larva feeds on trefoils and thymes.

Green-underside Blue *Glaucopsyche alexis* Wingspan 35mm

An active, open country butterfly. Males have violet-blue upper-wings with dark margins; female upperwings have much more extensive dark borders. The undersides of both sexes are similar and provide the best clues to identification: the background is plain brown and there are bands of bold dark spots, especially on the forewing, and greenish scaling at the base. Widespread but local in Europe, being absent from Britain, eastern Iberia and most of Scandinavia. It favours flowery grassland slopes and flies in April and May. Larval foodplants include vetches and brooms.

Large Blue *Maculinea arion* Wingspan 40mm

A local but widespread blue, best known for its larval association with ants. The upperwings are deep blue with dark margins. The male has a few dark markings on the upperwings while, in the female, these are more prominent. The underside is grey-brown with largish, prominent black spots and greenish-blue scales towards the wing base. Widely scattered colonies from northern Spain, across central France eastwards throughout Europe; it was declared extinct in Britain in 1979 but has been reintroduced since. It favours grassy banks including coastal cliffs and flies in July. The larval food-plant is Marjoram in western Europe and Thyme elsewhere.

Dusky Large Blue *Maculinea nausithous* Wingspan 40mm

A lowland butterfly, often associated with wetlands. The upperwings have a very dark blue colouring which instantly distinguishes this species from other Large Blues. There is a dark margin to both wings which, in females, is extremely extensive and extends along the fore-edge of the forewing. The underwing is also distinctive: the ground colour is chocolate brown with small dark spots and an unmarked margin. Occurs in a band from the French Savoie Alps eastwards through the Czech Republic and beyond. It is found in marshy areas and lakeland borders, flying in June. In its first two instars, the larva feeds on Great Burnet; thereafter it lives in an ant's nest.

Scarce Large Blue *Maculinea teleius* Wingspan 38mm

The smaller size and patterns of spots distinguish this species from the similar Large Blue. The upperwings of the male are pale blue while those of the female a darker hue; both sexes have a dark border and submarginal row of spots, both of which features are more pronounced in females than males. The underside is pale brown and unmarked except for a submarginal row of dark spots on each wing. Occurs from eastern France in a band eastwards that includes Switzerland and Austria. It favours damp meadows, sometimes up to 1,800m, and flies in June. The larva feeds on Great Burnet or Bird's-foot Trefoil in its first two instars; thereafter it lives in an ant's nest.

Baton Blue *Pseudophilotes baton* Wingspan 25mm

A mountain butterfly with distinctive markings. The upperwings of both sexes are blue and the margins are dark with chequered fringes. The underside is boldly speckled and there is a submarginal orange band on the hindwing. Has a range that covers northern Spain, mountain areas of France and stretches eastwards; the range excludes northern Europe and Britain. It is found at altitudes up to 1,800m and favours flowery banks where the larval foodplant, Wild Thyme, grows. When double-brooded, it flies in April and May, and again in August and September.

Panoptes Blue *Pseudophilotes panoptes* Wingspan 25mm

An attractive little upland butterfly. Considered by some to be a race of Baton Blue. The upperwings are deep blue, darker than those of the Baton Blue, and the margins are dark with chequered fringes. The underside is boldly speckled against a sooty-grey ground colour, darker than that of the Baton Blue; there is no submarginal orange band on the hindwing. Occurs in central and southern Spain. It flies at altitudes of around 1,000 to 1,500m and favours grassy slopes where the larval foodplant, Wild Thyme, flourishes. It has two broods, the first flying in April and May, the second in July.

Chequered Blue *Scolitantides orion* Wingspan 30mm

A very distinctive and attractive little butterfly. The upperwings are very dark but suffused with blue toward the wing base in both sexes; there is a submarginal white, scalloped line on each wing and the wing-fringes are chequered. The underside has a very pale ground colour and is beautifully marked with orange and black with chequered margins to the wings; the underwings recall the patterns on a Magpie Moth. Occurs as widely separated races in Sweden and in parts of eastern Spain, and from southern France eastwards. It favours mountain slopes where the larval foodplants, species of stonecrops, grow, and it flies from May to July.

Common Blue *Polyommatus icarus* Wingspan 32mm

One of the most common and widespread blues in Europe. Males have blue upperwings, the precise hue varying according to wear. Females have brown upperwings with varying amounts of blue and small, submarginal orange spots. The underside is grey-brown with dark spots, including one on the forewing cell; there are small, submarginal orange spots, best seen on the hindwing. Occurs throughout Europe. It flies in open spaces and grassland at almost all levels; it may even stray into parks and gardens, especially in hot years. It flies from April to October in successive broods and larval foodplants include clovers and trefoils.

Eros Blue *Polyommatus eros* Wingspan 30mm

A mountain butterfly with widely separated populations. The male has sky-blue upperwings with dark borders and dark veins radiating inwards. The female has brown upperwings, often with blue scaling at the wing base; there is usually either a submarginal band or orange crescentic spots. The underside is blue-grey with a pattern of dark spots characteristic of many blues; there is a spot in the cell of the forewing. Occurs in the Pyrenees, Alps, Apennines and locally in northern Greece. It favours grassy slopes above 2,000m and flies in July and August. The larva feeds on milk-vetches.

False Eros Blue *Polyommatus eroides* Wingspan 32mm

An attractive butterfly with a limited European range. Males have upperwings which are iridescent sky blue with pronounced black borders to the wings; females have plain brown upperwings and submarginal orange crescentic spots. The undersides are grey-brown with blue basal scaling and are well-marked with black spots; there are submarginal orange spots most pronounced on the hindwing. Also known as the Balkans Blue, occurs in the Balkans and has isolated populations in the Czech Republic. It favours upland meadows and flies in July.

Grizzled Skipper *Pyrgus malvae*
Wingspan 20mm

An attractively marked butterfly which rests with its wings outspread. The upperwings are dark brown, almost black, with numerous white spots and patches. On the underside, the dark ground colour is replaced by grey-brown on the forewing and tawny brown on the hindwing. The sexes are similar but the male has more angular wings. Occurs throughout Europe except northern Britain and northern Scandinavia; it is common in most of its range. It favours open country and grassy woodland edges, flying from April to August in two broods. Larval foodplants include rock-roses, Wild Strawberry and cinquefoils.

Alpine Grizzled Skipper *Pyrgus andromedae*
Wingspan 30mm

As its name suggests, an upland skipper. The upperwings are dark brown with a few white markings on the forewing, far fewer than on the Grizzled Skipper. The underwings are grey brown dotted with white spots and patches. Found in mountain ranges, occurring in the Alps, Pyrenees, northern Greece to Austria and northern Scandinavia. It prefers grassy hillsides and moors, usually above 1,500m in its more southerly sites, but lower in Scandinavia. It is on the wing in June and July and larval foodplants probably include cinquefoils.

Oberthur's Grizzled Skipper *Pyrgus armoricanus*
Wingspan 30mm

A widespread and often common skipper. Superficially very similar to the Grizzled Skipper but the white markings on the dark brown wings are always much less extensive and less intense, especially on the hindwings. The undersides are grey-brown on the forewing with a greenish tint to the hindwing; the pale band on the hindwing is more pronounced than in the Grizzled Skipper. Occurs across the whole of southern and central Europe north to a line running eastwards from southern Denmark. It is absent from Britain and Scandinavia. It favours flowery meadows and, in southern regions, flies from May to August in two broods.

Large Grizzled Skipper *Pyrgus alveus*
Wingspan 30mm

A common and widespread butterfly. The upperwings are smoky grey in the male and brown in the female; this species has perhaps the least extensive or pronounced white markings of any common member of this potentially confusing group of Skippers. The underwings are olive-brown and show white markings including a distinct white band on the hindwing. Absent from Britain and Scandinavia but otherwise found throughout Europe. It favours grassland and flies from June to August in one extended brood. Larval foodplants include rock-roses, Wild Strawberry and cinquefoils.

Safflower Skipper *Pyrgus carthami* (*fritillarius*)
Wingspan 32mm

A common and widespread skipper. At first glance, resembles an out-size Grizzled Skipper. The upperwings are sooty-grey with prominent white markings; those spots on the hindwing near the margin form a broken band. The underwings are yellow-olive with conspicuous white markings, the margins of which are defined with dark scaling, especially on the hindwing; they form three, irregular bands. Occurs throughout southern and central Europe but is absent from north-west Europe including Britain, and from Scandinavia. It favours meadows and flies from July to September in an extended brood. The larva feeds on cinquefoils and mallows.

Carline Skipper *Pyrgus carlinae*
Wingspan 30mm

A mountain butterfly with a restricted distribution. The upperwings are sooty grey-brown with small white flecks and markings on the forewings but the pale markings on the hindwing are reduced or absent. The underside is olive-green with conspicuous white markings on the hindwing forming at least one short but broad band. Found only in southern and western parts of the Alps. It favours Alpine meadows, generally around or above 2,000m, where the larval foodplant, Spring Cinquefoil, grows. It is on the wing in July and August.

104

Dusky Grizzled Skipper *Pyrgus cacaliae*
Wingspan 30mm

An active, but sun-loving high Alpine butterfly. The upperwings are dark sooty-brown with small white flecks on the forewing and almost no pale markings on the hindwing. The underside is olive brown and there are large, somewhat diffuse white markings on the hindwing and white markings on the forewing similar to those on its upper surface. Found in the Alps eastwards from the Alpes Maritimes, the Pyrenees and very locally in the Balkans. It favours high Alpine meadows above an altitude of 2,000m. The butterfly is on the wing in July and August in a single brood and the larva feeds on Coltsfoot.

Red-underwing Skipper *Spialia sertorius*
Wingspan 20 to 25mm

A widespread and variable skipper, superficially similar to the Grizzled Skipper. The upperwings are dark brown or almost black with variable white markings on both wings. The underwings show more extensive white markings against a reddish ground colour on the hindwings and a grey-brown ground colour on the forewing. Sexes are similar. Occurs across most of southern and central Europe from Iberia to Greece; absent from north-west Europe including Britain. It flies in grassy places up to about 1,000m and is on the wing in two broods from April to August. Larval foodplants include cinquefoils.

Tessellated Skipper *Syrichtus tessellum* Wingspan 35mm

A comparatively large skipper with a limited European range and one of several potentially confusing species that are similar to one another. At a glance, it resembles a large specimen of Grizzled Skipper. The upperwings are dark grey-brown with well-defined white markings on both wings. The underside is yellow-olive with well-defined white markings forming three bands on the hindwing. Found in Greece and neighbouring regions in the Balkans. It occurs in flower-rich meadows and has a single brood, flying in May and June.

Sage Skipper *Syrichtus proto* Wingspan 25mm

An active little southern European butterfly. The upperwings are dark grey-brown with small white markings scattered over the forewings and forming a short band on the hindwing; the markings vary in intensity, however. The underside shows yellowish-grey scaling on the hindwing with large pale spots; the forewing shows more contrast between the dark ground colour and white markings. Occurs in warmer regions of southern Europe including most of Iberia, and locally in southern France, Italy and Greece. It favours grassy slopes up to around 1,500m and flies in May and June. The larva feeds on sages.

Dingy Skipper *Erynnis tages* Wingspan 25mm

A rather sombre butterfly that sometimes rests like a moth with wings outspread, or with the wings closed, tent-like over the body. The upperwings are dark grey-brown with darker markings. The underwings are more reddish-brown with a faint speckling of pale spots. The sexes are similar but males have more angular wings. Occurs throughout Europe including Britain but is absent from northern Scandinavia. It is often common in open, grassy country and rough, scrubby places, flying from May to August. Larval foodplants include Bird's-foot Trefoil and various vetches.

Mallow Skipper *Carcharodus alceae* Wingspan 30mm

A widespread but rather nondescript skipper. The upperwings are dark, dingy brown with faint dark markings on both wings and small white markings on the forewings. The underside is grey-brown with more extensive white flecks and patches. The sexes are similar. Found throughout most of central and southern Europe from a line eastwards from Brittany and south to the Mediterranean; it is absent from Britain. It favours grassy hillsides where its larval foodplants (various species of mallows) flourish. There are two or more broods, butterflies being seen from April to August.

Marbled Skipper *Carcharodus lavatherae*
Wingspan 32mm

One of the more readily recognisable members of this confusing group of skippers. The upperwings are marbled with white and dark brown patterns but the dark areas are suffused with olive or yellow scaling giving a rather pale, dusty appearance. The underside is very pale greenish-yellow with faint white markings, looking altogether bleached. Occurs widely across southern and south-eastern Europe, except in Iberia where it is confined to central and southern upland regions. It flies in grassy places from May onwards in two or more broods. Larval foodplants include White Horehound.

Large Chequered Skipper *Heteropterus morpheus*
Wingspan 30mm

A very active butterfly in warm weather with drab upperwings but beautifully marked beneath. The upperwings are dark brown with a few yellow-buff markings on the forewing. The underwings have a ground colour of yellow-buff and show large, black-ringed, white oval spots. The sexes are similar but the female has more pronounced yellow markings on the forewing and chequered fringes. Range includes western France, parts of northern Spain, Italy, Germany and much of eastern Europe. It is a lowland species, occurring in light, grassy woodland and flying in June and July. The larva feeds on grasses.

Chequered Skipper *Carterocephalus palaemon*
Wingspan 25mm

A beautifully marked skipper. The upperwings are rich dark brown with bold yellow markings giving a chequered effect. The underwing patterns reflect those of the upper surface but the dark ground colour is replaced by grey-brown on the hindwing and is effectively reversed on the forewing. Range includes most of France and central Europe; it occurs in northern Scandinavia but is absent from the south and from most of Spain and Italy. In Britain, it recently became extinct in England but has thriving colonies in western Scotland. It flies in light woodland in May and June and the larva feeds on grasses.

Lulworth Skipper *Thymelicus acteon*
Wingspan 25mm

An active little skipper with distinctively coloured wings. The upperwings are variable in ground colour but are usually khaki in males, their forewings showing an oblique scent brand and a subtly paler ring of spots, rather like a paw-print. In the larger female, the forewing ring of spots is more conspicuous and pale orange. Occurs across much of Europe, including southern England (mainly the Dorset coast); it is absent from north-east Europe and Scandinavia. It favours grassy slopes and cliff tops, and flies from May to July. The larval foodplants are grasses.

109

Essex Skipper *Thymelicus lineolus*
Wingspan 25mm

A colourful and engaging little butterfly. It is almost indistinguishable from the Small Skipper except for the black spots on the underside of the antennae. The upperwings are orange-brown with a dark margin; males show an oblique sex brand on the forewing. The underside is buffish-brown on the hindwing and orange-brown on the forewing. Occurs across most of Europe except northern Britain and northern Scandinavia. It flies in long grasses, frequently visiting flowers such as Marjoram, and is seen from May to August. The larva feeds on grasses.

Small Skipper *Thymelicus sylvestris* Wingspan 25mm

Often extremely common during the summer months. It is very similar to the Essex Skipper but the tips of the antennae are orange-brown not black. The upperwings are orange-brown with a dark margin; males have a prominent sex brand, more conspicuous than male Essex Skippers. The underwings are grey-brown on the hindwing and orange-brown on the forewing. Occurs throughout Europe except most of Scandinavia and the north of England. It favours grassy areas, visiting thistle and knapweed flowers, and flies from May to September. The larva feeds on soft grasses.

Silver-spotted Skipper *Hesperia comma*
Wingspan 25mm

A mainly chalk downland butterfly with attractively marked underwings. It can be confused with the Large Skipper and the best identification features are the silvery-white spots on the greenish underwings, most noticeable on the hindwing. The upperwings are dark brown with orange-buff markings and spots; males have a dark sex brand. Occurs locally across much of Europe except northern Scandinavia; in Britain, it is confined to a few colonies on short-cropped turf in southern England. It prefers chalk or limestone grassland and flies in July and August. The larva feeds on grasses.

Large Skipper *Ochlodes venatus* Wingspan 25mm

A common and familiar grassland butterfly. The upperwings are orange-brown, certainly more orange than the Silver-spotted Skipper; the male has a dark sex brand and the female has brighter spotting on the forewing and hindwing. The underside is buffish-orange and both wings have subtle, paler spotting. The Large Skipper occurs throughout Europe except the south coast of Spain and northern Scandinavia; it is found up to 2,000m in some areas. It occurs in grassland of all kinds and flies in June and July; in the south more broods may occur. The larva feeds on a variety of grasses.

Lime Hawk Moth *Mimas tiliae* Wingspan 65mm

A large and attractive moth with beautifully marked wings. At rest, the hindwings are partly concealed by the forewings and this affords it excellent camouflage when resting among leaves. The wing margins are irregular and the upperwings have a greenish or pinkish-buff ground colour. The margins of the forewing are darker with a pale patch at the tip and there are two dark patches on the forewing, one larger than the other. Common in most parts of Europe where the larval foodplants, mainly species of lime and elm, grow. It flies in May and June and comes to lights. The dull green larva has oblique stripes on its body and a bluish horn at the tail end.

Poplar Hawk Moth *Laothoe populi* Wingspan 80mm

A large, night-flying moth with subtly marked wings. The ground colour of the upperwings varies from lilac-brown to grey-brown. There is a dark band across the forewing and broken, dark lines across both wings; on the hindwing there is a conspicuous reddish-maroon spot near the base. The body and base of the wings are silky hairy. At rest, the forewings partly conceal the hindwings. If disturbed, however, they may be spread to reveal the red spot. Widespread in Europe except the far north, flying in May and June. The larva is an attractive green colour with oblique stripes and a tail horn; it feeds on various species of poplars and willows.

112

Eyed Hawk Moth *Smerinthus ocellata* Wingspan 80mm

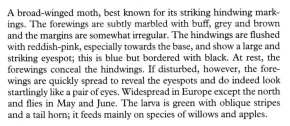

A broad-winged moth, best known for its striking hindwing markings. The forewings are subtly marbled with buff, grey and brown and the margins are somewhat irregular. The hindwings are flushed with reddish-pink, especially towards the base, and show a large and striking eyespot; this is blue but bordered with black. At rest, the forewings conceal the hindwings. If disturbed, however, the forewings are quickly spread to reveal the eyespots and do indeed look startlingly like a pair of eyes. Widespread in Europe except the north and flies in May and June. The larva is green with oblique stripes and a tail horn; it feeds mainly on species of willows and apples.

Death's-head Hawk Moth *Acherontia atropos* Wingspan 110mm

A large and striking moth, best known for the skull and crossbone (death's-head) marking on its thorax. The forewings are dark but subtly marbled with buff, yellow and brown. The hindwings are yellow with bands of black. The abdomen is marked with yellow and black. When alarmed, the moth can hiss loudly. Widespread in southern and central Europe as far as central France. It is not resident in Britain, but this strong migrant is sometimes recorded as a vagrant and occasionally breeds. In southern Europe, it can be found from May onwards until the autumn. The huge larva, which is yellow with blue stripes, is sometimes found feeding on potato leaves.

113

Convolvulus Hawk Moth *Agrius convolvuli*
Wingspan 110mm

A large and fast-flying moth with narrow wings. The forewings are subtly marked with grey and brown providing an excellent camouflage when against tree bark. The hindwings are greyish-buff and have bands of darker scaling. There are pink, white and black bands on the abdomen; these are often hidden by the wings at rest. Widespread in southern Europe but less numerous in central Europe. It is not resident in Britain but migrants are sometimes recorded in the late summer. In southern Europe, it can be seen from May onwards. The moth often visits the flowers of tobacco plants in gardens, hovering as it feeds and using its incredibly long proboscis.

Privet Hawk Moth *Sphinx ligustri* Wingspan 100mm

A large and impressive moth. The forewings are brown but streaked and marbled with buff and black. The hindwings have pale and dark bands with a pinkish tinge toward the base. The centre of the abdomen is pale, the segments are marked with pink and black bands. Widespread in southern and central Europe; its range extends to southern Britain and southern Scandinavia. The large green larva has oblique purple and white stripes and a tail horn. It feeds mainly on privet but will also occur on lilac in gardens. The moth flies in June and July.

114

Pine Hawk Moth *Hyloicus pinastri*
Wingspan 85mm

A narrow-winged, fast-flying moth. The upperwings are grey-brown and have subtle, dark bands on the forewings and are stippled with dark brown. The overall effect is to produce a wonderful bark-like appearance which is seen to best effect when the moth rests camouflaged on the trunks of pine trees. Widespread in southern and central Europe; it appears to have colonised southern Britain over the last century. It flies in May and June and will visit Honeysuckle flowers and sometimes comes to lights. The larva feeds on pine needles.

Spurge Hawk Moth *Hyles euphorbiae* Wingspan 80mm

An attractive, mainly southern European moth. The forewings are olive brown with a broad and irregular pale stripe and a pale margin. The hindwings have a deep pink band, bordered by black; the trailing margin of the wing is pale. Widespread in southern and central Europe but absent as a resident from Britain. Since the moths are powerful fliers and dispersive, a few are recorded in Britain from time to time. As its name implies, the larva feeds on various species of spurges; it is beautifully marked with yellow and red dots against a black ground colour.

Bedstraw Hawk Moth *Hyles gallii*
Wingspan 75mm

An attractive moth, superficially similar to the Spurge Hawk Moth. Like this latter species, it too has olive-brown forewings but the pale stripe is narrower and better defined. On the hindwing, there is a broad, pale stripe which is flushed with deep pink towards the base. It occurs throughout most of Europe but is absent from Britain as a resident; it does, however, occur as a rare vagrant. The moth is on the wing in May and June and lays its eggs on the leaves of bedstraws. In warm climates, it is occasionally seen feeding on the wing at dusk but is otherwise strictly nocturnal.

Striped Hawk Moth *Hyles lineata livornica* Wingspan 80mm

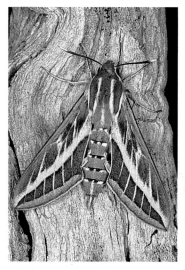

A strikingly marked and fast-flying moth. The forewings are olive-brown with a well-defined pale bar and pale, narrow stripes marking the veins. The hindwing has a pale pink band that is clearly defined by broad, brown bands. At rest, the stripes run parallel with the body. It is essentially a warm-climate insect and is most numerous in southern Europe. Its range does, however, extend into central Europe and it occasionally reaches Britain, sometimes producing larvae; these feed on vines and fuchsias. The moths fly from May to August and can sometimes be seen feeding at dusk, especially during warm weather.

Silver-striped Hawk Moth *Hippotion celerio*
Wingspan 75mm

An attractive, fast-flying moth that is occasionally seen feeding on the wing during the daytime. The forewings are brown with bark-like patterns of buff and black; there is a prominent and conspicuous silvery-white stripe through the wings. The hindwings are flushed with deep pink at the base and have radiating dark veins over a pale pink band. Common and widespread in southern Europe, especially around the Mediterranean. Its range does, however, extend into parts of central Europe and, on occasions, it has reached as far north as Britain. The moth flies from May to September and the larva feeds on bedstraws and vines.

Oleander Hawk Moth *Daphnis nerii* Wingspan 95mm

An extremely attractive, southern European hawk moth. The narrow wings are beautifully patterned and mottled with various shades of green, pink, lilac and brown; green is the dominant colour. A warm climate insect, which is most numerous around the Mediterranean. Its range does, however, extend northwards into southern Europe and on rare occasions it even reaches British shores. The moth flies mainly from June to September and the greenish larva feeds mostly on Oleander, a common Mediterranean shrub. The moth is sometimes seen visiting flowers at dusk.

Small Elephant Hawk Moth *Deilephila porcellus*
Wingspan 50mm

A beautiful but unobtrusive moth. The forewings and hindwings are pinkish but with broad, yellow to olive bands across them. The body of the moth is also pinkish and densely hairy. Occurs almost throughout southern and central Europe, including most of Britain. It is on the wing in May and June and is sometimes seen visiting the flowers of Honeysuckle. The larva, after which the moth gets its name, is brown with eyespots near the head end; when alarmed, the body is contracted, expanding the eyes and creating the impression of an elephant's head and trunk. It feeds on bedstraws.

Elephant Hawk Moth *Deilephila elpenor*
Wingspan 65mm

An attractive and often common hawk moth. The forewings are pink but are flushed with olive-yellow scaling and bear an oblique pale stripe. The hindwings are bright pink with the leading edge and base black. The body of the moth is pink with olive lengthways side stripes. It is found throughout Europe including Britain as far north as southern Scotland; it flies in June. The remarkable larva, which feeds on willowherbs, is green or brown with large eyespots near the head end. These are expanded when alarmed, and the head end is waved about like an elephant's trunk.

Hummingbird Hawk Moth *Macroglossum stellatarum*
Wingspan 45mm

In southern Europe, this is a familiar day-flying moth, sometimes even mistakenly taken for a real hummingbird. The forewings are dark brown with black transverse lines. The hindwings are orange with dark bases and borders. Widespread in central and southern Europe. It is not resident in Britain, but in the warmer months (June to August) it spreads northwards and is fairly regularly encountered in southern England. The unobtrusive larva feeds on various species of bedstraws. The moth is seen hovering around flowers such as Red Valerian, feeding on nectar with its long tongue.

Broad-bordered Bee Hawk Moth *Hemaris fuciformis*
Wingspan 40mm

An intriguing and unusual hawk moth that resembles a bumble-bee more than a moth. Newly emerged specimens have scale-covered wings but these are soon lost. The forewings and hind-wings are mostly transparent but have broad, reddish borders and dark veins. The body of the moth is light brown and furry with a reddish 'waist' band. Widespread in Europe and locally common in southern Britain. It is a day-flying species, visiting flowers such as Bugle and Ground Ivy, mostly in the mornings, and feeding on the wing. The larva feeds on Honeysuckle.

Sallow Kitten *Furcula furcula* Wingspan 35mm

A delicately marked moth. The forewings are greyish-white marked with a dark central band; the edges of the band are flushed with orange and outlined with black. There are dark spots on the margin of the wing. The hindwing is white. The moth is sometimes found resting on sallows when the wings often embrace the twig that it is resting upon. The Sallow Kitten is found across central and northern Europe including most of Britain. It flies in June and the eggs are laid on the leaves of Sallow and other species of willow. The larva is green and plump with two flexible tail projections.

Puss Moth *Cerura vinula* Wingspan 70mm

A large, hairy moth which is best known for its extraordinary larva. The upperwings are greyish-white and the scales are etched in black; there are often faint grey lines and marks between the veins. The body is cloaked in long, fluffy white hairs. Occurs widely throughout Europe and is found more-or-less throughout Britain. It flies in May and June and the eggs are laid on species of willow and poplar. The larva is large, plump and green with a brown band on the back and two long 'tails'. Keen-eyed observers may find the moth resting during the daytime on the bark of trees.

120

Lobster Moth *Stauropus fagi* Wingspan 55m

A sizeable moth, better known and named for the appearance of its larva rather than the adult. The upperwings are grey-brown and subtly marked and marbled with buff and black; there is usually a salmon-pink flush towards the wing base. The body of the moth is extremely hairy and males have feathered antennae. Widespread in central Europe and parts of the south; in Britain, it occurs mainly in southern England. The Lobster Moth flies in May and June and the eggs are laid on beech, oak and other trees. When fully grown, the larva fancifully resembles a lobster, or perhaps more realistically a praying mantis.

Lesser Swallow Prominent *Pheosia gnoma* Wingspan 40mm

A medium-sized moth with smooth, curved wing margins. The forewings are marked with white and dark brown shading, a dark mark near the wingtip and a dark trailing margin; there is also a white wedge-shaped mark, the best means of distinguishing this species from the similar Swallow Prominent *P. tremula*. The underwings are pale, shading to dark at the margins; at rest, the underwings are concealed by the forewings. Widespread in Europe, including Britain. It flies in May and June, and the larva feeds on birch.

121

Iron Prominent *Notodonta dromedarius* Wingspan 35mm

At rest, this species, in the manner of other prominents, shows a small but noticeable hump or prominence on its back when seen in profile. The forewings are dark brown but marked with rust-coloured lines and patches. The hindwings are pale grey-brown but are completely concealed at rest. It is widespread in Europe and occurs throughout most of Britain. It is a moth of mature woodland and it flies in May and June. The eggs are laid mainly on the leaves of birch and alder. The larva is green and has bumps or prominences on its back and at its tail end.

Pale Prominent *Pterostoma palpina* Wingspan 40mm

When seen at rest, this moth closely resembles a frayed piece of wood, a deception that is usually employed to good effect while at rest in the daytime. The wings are buffish-brown in colour with dark streaks and irregular bands that help create the wood-like appearance. The effect is further enhanced by the moth's bumpy profile and by its legs being thrust forward at rest. Widespread throughout central and northern Europe, including the southern regions of Britain where it is locally common. It is a woodland moth which flies in May and June. The larva feeds on poplars and willows.

Buff-tip *Phalera bucephala* Wingspan 60mm

An attractive and aptly named moth. The forewings are silvery-grey with dark and white scaling giving the appearance of birch bark; there is a scalloped buff tip to the wing. The hindwings are pale and are concealed at rest. When at rest, the moth bears more than a passing resemblance to a broken birch twig. Occurs across central and northern Europe and is found in most parts of Britain. It is primarily a woodland moth but also occurs in mature gardens. It flies in June and July and the semi-colonial larvae feed on the leaves of almost any species of tree or shrub, but particularly lime or hazel.

Chocolate-tip *Clostera curtula* Wingspan 30mm

Despite its small size, this is a most attractive moth when viewed in close up. The forewings are grey-brown with transverse pale lines dividing the wing into quarters; the tip of the wing is a rich maroon-chocolate. The hindwing is pale and concealed at rest. The colour of the wingtip is also picked up on the head and on the tip of the abdomen; if the moth is alarmed, this is sometimes reflexed. Widespread in central and northern Europe; in Britain, mainly found in the south. It is a woodland moth which flies in two broods, April and May, and then July and August. The larva feeds on Aspen and poplars.

Buff Arches *Habrosyne pyritoides* Wingspan 35mm

A most attractive moth whose markings provide good camouflage among fallen leaves and bark. The forewings have a triangular area of orange-brown with bark-like markings; this is outlined with white lines with smooth-looking grey-brown areas on the remaining part of the wing. The overall effect is of a piece of wood from which the bark has peeled in places. The hindwings are greyish and concealed at rest. Widespread in central Europe; in Britain, it is widespread and locally common in most wooded regions. The moth flies in June and July and the larva feeds mainly on bramble leaves.

Peach-blossom *Thyatira batis* Wingspan 35mm

A beautiful and well-named moth. The forewings are greenish-brown marbled with darker markings and displaying five pinkish-white spots on each wing. These do indeed bear a passing resemblance to the blossom of fruit trees but may well serve to camouflage the moth among leafy lichens. The hindwings are grey-brown and are concealed at rest. Occurs across central and northern Europe; in Britain, it occurs as far north as southern Scotland. It is a woodland species and the moth flies in June. The larva feeds mainly on the leaves of bramble.

Yellow-tail *Euproctis similis* Wingspan 35mm

An extremely hairy, white moth, all stages of which can cause serious irritations with its poisonous hairs. The upperwings are pure white and the body of the moth carries long hairs. These resemble the downy plumes of a feather and this is what the moth is sometimes overlooked as. Occurs widely in central Europe; in Britain, it is found mainly in the southern counties of England. The moth is on the wing in June and July and favours areas of woodland and scrub. The silken tents, in which the young larvae live and overwinter, are sometimes seen in bushes of hawthorn and other hedgerow shrubs.

Lackey *Malacosoma neustria* Wingspan 35mm

A relatively small and active moth perhaps best known for the silken tents in which its gregarious larvae live and on which they are sometimes seen basking in the sun. The wings are buffish-brown and the forewings are marked with two dark lines. Occurs across central Europe and is locally common; in Britain, it is found mainly in southern England. It is a moth of hedgerows and wood-land, flying in July and August. The larvae, which feed on hedgerow shrubs such as Blackthorn and Hawthorn, are marked with blue, red and white and are most conspicuous in early spring.

125

Drinker *Philudoria potatoria* Wingspan 55mm

A large and attractive moth of wetlands and grasslands. The wings are buffish and the veins are highlighted in darker brown; there is an oblique darker line on the forewing. At rest, the hindwings are concealed and the forewings are usually held at an angle over the body. Widespread in Europe and is found throughout much of Britain, flying in July. It prefers damp habitats where grasses, the foodplants of the larva, flourish. The larva, which is brown and hairy, is also known to drink drops of water, hence the moth's name.

Lappet Moth *Gastropacha quercifolia* Wingspan 60 to 70mm

A superb leaf-mimic which is easily overlooked. The upperwings are a rich reddish-brown colour. The margins are scalloped and there are scalloped marks forming lines across the wings. At rest, the moth holds its wings in such a fashion as to complement the cryptic colouring and create a convincing impression of a dead, fallen leaf. Widespread in Europe and in Britain is found commonly in England. It flies in June and July and the eggs are laid on hedgerow shrubs, particularly Hawthorn. The larva is one of the largest in Europe. It is as easy to overlook as the adult, however, since it can wrap itself lengthways around twigs.

126

Emperor Moth *Pavonia pavonia* Wingspan 55 to 70mm

One of Europe's most distinctive and attractive moths, its recognition made easier by its day-flying habits. Males are smaller than females and have feathery rather than filamentous antennae. There is a striking eyespot on all wings and the forewings are greyish while the hindwings are orange; the wing margins are pale but shaded to give a feeling of depth. The female has similar wing patterns to the male but is lilac-grey. Widespread in central and northern Europe. In Britain, it is more-or-less confined to areas of heath and moor where the main larval foodplant, Ling, grows. It flies in April and May.

Green Silver Lines *Pseudoips fagana* Wingspan 35mm

A most attractive moth with a very descriptive name. The forewings are bright green and are scribed by three silvery-white oblique lines. The hindwings are pale and are concealed at rest. Widespread in central and northern Europe; in Britain, it occurs as far north as southern Scotland and is locally common. It is a moth of woodland and scrub which flies in June and July. The larva feeds on a variety of trees and shrubs including hazel, oak and birch. The green coloration of the forewings provides excellent camouflage when the moth is resting.

White Ermine *Spilosoma lubricipeda* Wingspan 40mm

Another extremely aptly named moth and one which is fairly common. The forewings are off-white and speckled with black spots, resembling ermine in appearance. The hindwings are pure white and unmarked except for a couple of black spots; at rest, the hindwings remain concealed. Widespread in central and northern Europe and occurs across much of Britain. It is a moth of woodland edge, hedgerow and scrubby grassland and flies in June. The moth is sometimes attracted to house lights in rural areas. The larva feeds on a wide range of herbaceous plants.

Garden Tiger Moth *Arctia caja* Wingspan 60 to 70mm

A distinctive and attractive moth and one which is familiar to many people. The forewings are creamy white with well-defined patterns of chocolate-brown, recalling the markings on a leopard's coat. The underwings are bright orange with a varying number of large, black spots. The moth's abdomen is also bright orange with black marks. Occurs across most of Europe and is found more-or-less throughout Britain. It flies in July and August and is often attracted to street or house lights. The hairy caterpillars, known as 'woolly bears' feed on a wide range of herbaceous plants.

Jersey Tiger Moth *Euplagia quadripunctaria* Wingspan 55mm

An attractive moth sometimes encountered during the daytime. The forewings are dark brown with two conspicuous white stripes across the wing as well as other white markings. The hindwings, which are concealed when the moth is at rest, are orange-red with three or more black spots. Widespread in central and southern Europe; in Britain, it is known mostly from the south. Perhaps best known on the Greek island of Rhodes where thousands collect in a damp, wooded valley, inappropriately named the 'Valley of the Butterflies', during the dry, hot summer. The moth generally flies in July and August.

Ruby Tiger Moth *Phragmatobia fuliginosa* Wingspan 30mm

An attractive little moth that readily comes to moth traps and occasionally to house lights. The forewings are rather variable but are usually deep ruby-red in colour; they can be much darker, however. The hindwings are bluish with a red tone but are usually concealed when the moth is resting. The Ruby Tiger Moth is widespread across central Europe and occurs throughout most of Britain. It is a moth of wayside, hedgerow and woodland and flies in July. The larva feeds on a wide range of low-growing herbaceous plants.

Cinnabar Moth *Tyria jacobaeae* Wingspan 40mm

An attractive and distinctive moth that is often seen flying in the late afternoon and at dusk. The forewings are dark greyish-brown with a red stripe and two red spots. The hindwings are red with a dark margin. Widespread in Europe and, in Britain, occurs as far north as central Scotland. It is a moth of waysides and fields and flies in May and June. The species is equally well known for its colourful larvae which are striped orange and black to advertise their distasteful nature to birds. They are often seen in clusters on the foodplant, Ragwort, which they strip bare.

Common Footman *Eilema lurideola* Wingspan 35mm

The footman moths are a curious group which characteristically rest with their slender wings slightly rolled around their bodies. This elongated appearance and their habit of walking when disturbed makes them appear superficially like caddis-flies. The forewing of this species is sooty-grey all over with a yellowish leading edge. The hindwing is yellowish-buff. It is widespread across Europe and, in Britain, is found in most parts of the country except the north of Scotland. It flies in July and is a moth of waysides and hedgerows. The larva will eat lichens and various hedgerow plants.

Grey Dagger *Acronicta psi* Wingspan 40mm

An attractive and often common moth. The forewings are rather variable in ground colour but are usually soft grey; the wings are subtly marbled with darker scaling and have three striking black markings, two of which at least resemble daggers. The hindwings are pale and are usually concealed when the moth is at rest. It is widespread across Europe and is found in most parts of Britain. It is a moth of woodlands and hedgerows and generally flies in June, often being attracted to lights and moth traps. The larva feeds on a variety of shrubs and trees including Hawthorn, birch and sallow.

Heart and Dart *Agrotis exclamationis* Wingspan 35mm

An extremely common and widespread moth and one which is subject to considerable variation. Typical specimens have light brown to dark brown forewings with two dark markings, one resembling a heart, the other a dart. The hindwings are grey and usually concealed when the moth is resting. There are other similar species but this one usually has a dark marking at the front of the thorax. Widespread in central Europe and occurs throughout Britain as far as southern Scotland. It is found in fields, hedgerows and gardens and flies in June and July. The larva feeds on a wide range of low-growing, herbaceous plants.

The Shark *Cucullia umbratica* Wingspan 50mm

An unusual moth with wing patterning that makes it resemble a piece of chipped wood. The upperwings are buffish-brown in colour but are streaked and veined with darker brown in a pattern that resembles cut wood; the moth usually sits on an appropriate substrate during the day. The forewings are more marked than the hindwings which are usually concealed when the moth is resting. Found in central Europe including Britain where it occurs in most regions. It is a moth of woodland and hedgerow and is on the wing in June and July. The larva feeds on a variety of herbaceous plants.

Angle Shades *Phlogophora meticulosa* Wingspan 45mm

An attractive and familiar moth, appropriately named. The forewings are greenish-brown and buffish with angular darker markings of reddish-brown. The hindwings are pale. When resting, the forewings conceal the hindwings and are characteristically folded and look crumpled. Common and widespread in Europe including Britain. It generally flies from July to September but often later. The larva feeds on a range of herbaceous plants, including ones in gardens. Potted geraniums, left outdoors during the summer months and brought indoors in autumn, often yield moths late in the year.

Burnished Brass *Diachrysia chrysitis* Wingspan 35mm

Despite its relatively small size, this is one of the more attractive moths in the whole of Europe. The forewings are brown but burnished with bands of metallic, golden-yellow that glints in the light. The hindwings are brown and usually concealed when the moth is resting. It is widespread in central Europe and, in Britain, it is found mainly in southern England. It is a moth of woodland and hedgerows and flies during June and July. Old specimens sometimes lose their metallic lustre through wear. The larva feeds on herbaceous plants such as the Common Nettle.

Beautiful Golden Y *Autographa pulchrina* Wingspan 35mm

An attractive and common moth. The forewings are richly coloured with orange-brown, grey-brown and chocolate in bands and mottled patterns. There are two, conspicuous pale marks on the wing, one a spot, the other resembling a V or a U; taken together, they form the Y in the moth's name. The hindwings are pale grey-buff and are concealed when the moth is resting. Widespread in central Europe including most of Britain. It is a moth of fields and waysides, flying in June and July. The larva feeds on a variety of herbaceous plants such as nettles and plantains.

Silver Y *Autographa gamma* Wingspan 40mm

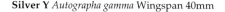

An active and easily disturbed moth which is often seen flying in the daytime, visiting flowers to feed. The forewings are attractively mottled and marbled with brown, buff, grey and black; the moth gets its name from the conspicuous silvery-white Y marking on the forewing. The hindwing is pale buffish-grey with a dark margin. Widespread in Europe and particularly common in the south. In Britain, it is seen mainly as a migrant, the moths first arriving in June and July, sometimes in considerable numbers. The larva feeds on a range of low-growing, herbaceous plants.

Mother Shipton *Callistege mi* Wingspan 30mm

A distinctive day-flying moth which could easily be mistaken for a butterfly. The forewings are grey-brown and marked with pale and dark patterns that fancifully resemble the facial profile of the haggard folklore witch after which the moth is named. The hindwings are barred with orange-buff and dark brown. Widespread in central and northern Europe, in Britain being found in most regions except the north of Scotland. It occurs in fields and hedgerows, flying mainly in May and June. The larva feeds on a variety of low-growing plants.

Herald *Scoliopteryx libatrix* Wingspan 40mm

An attractive moth, unusual in that it hibernates. The forewings are buffish-brown and grey-brown, scribed with white lines, these lines defining regions of orange-red towards the base. The hind-wings are brown but are usually concealed when the moth is at rest. Widespread in Europe and is found throughout most of Britain. The moth generally emerges in September and October and then hibernates in outbuildings, roof spaces and in dense ivy; it reappears in the following spring. It is a species of woodlands, waysides and gardens and the larva feeds on willows and poplars.

Red Underwing *Catocala nupta* Wingspan 70mm

A large moth with superbly camouflaged forewings but striking hind-wings. The forewings are beautifully marked with grey and brown producing an effect that resembles tree bark; when the moth is rest-ing on the trunk of a poplar or willow, or indeed even a wooden fence, it can be very difficult to spot. Occurs across Europe and, in Britain, occurs mainly in the south of England. It is a moth of wooded areas or even mature gardens, flying in August and September. The larva feeds on willows and sallows and is extremely well camouflaged when it rests pressed close to a twig.

Magpie Moth *Abraxes grossulariata*
Wingspan 35mm

A striking and easily recognisable moth which is often disturbed from hedgerows or garden vegetation during the daytime. The markings on the upperwings are extremely variable but typical specimens have a white ground colour and a well-defined pattern of black spots and an orange-yellow flush between two rows of spots on the forewing and also at the wing base. The hindwing does not have so many spots as the forewing. Widespread in central and northern Europe and occurs across most of Britain. It flies in July and August and is found in waysides and woodland edges. The larva feeds on a variety of hedgerow plants such as Hawthorn.

Purple Thorn *Selenia tetralunaria* Wingspan 35mm

One of several rather similar species of moths, all of which superficially resemble dead leaves. The upperwings and underwings are rather similar in appearance: they are marbled and mottled with purplish brown and pinkish buff with concentric dark lines. The moth characteristically rests with its wings folded over its body. Widespread in central and northern Europe; it is widespread and locally common in Britain. Favoured habitats include woodlands and hedgerows and the moth flies in two broods, the first in April and May, and the second in August. The larva feeds on a variety of trees and shrubs including oak, birch and sallow.

136

Swallowtail Moth *Ourapteryx sambucaria*
Wingspan 55mm

An attractive and easily recognisable moth, somewhat butterfly-like in appearance. It is easily disturbed from wayside vegetation along hedgerows and in scrub during the daytime; it also comes to house lights. The wings, which are pointed and bear small tail streamers on the hindwings, are lemon-yellow; there are faint dark transverse lines, mainly seen on the forewing. The Swallowtail is widespread in central Europe and, in Britain, it is commonest in the south. It is a woodland moth and flies in May and June. The twig-like larva moves by looping its body and feeds on hedgerow shrubs such as Hawthorn.

Brimstone Moth *Opisthograptis luteolata* Wingspan 35mm

An attractive and distinctive moth which is widespread and often common. The upperwings are brimstone-yellow and there are faint dark markings on the wings and rich chestnut along the leading edge of the forewing. The Brimstone is widespread in central and northern Europe; in Britain, it is found in most wooded regions. It is a woodland and hedgerow moth which flies mostly in May and June, but also more occasionally later in the year. The larva is twig-like and is easily overlooked as it rests on its foodplants which include Blackthorn and Hawthorn.

Speckled Yellow *Pseudopanthera macularia*
Wingspan 30mm

One look at this attractive moth and the observer will realise that it has an extremely descriptive name. The upperwings are deep yellow in colour and are speckled with dots and patches of chestnut brown; both forewings and hindwings are so marked. Widespread in central Europe and, in Britain, occurs widely although it is commonest in the south. It favours woodlands and scrub and is on the wing in June. It flies during the daytime and often settles on bramble leaves. The larva feeds on Wood-sage and related members of the mint family.

Five-spot Burnet *Zygaena trifolii* Wingspan 35mm

A colourful and distinctive day-flying moth. The upperwings are dark, with a greenish metallic sheen and five red spots. The hindwings are red with a broad dark border. It is widespread in Europe and, in Britain, occurs mostly in southern regions. It is a meadow-loving moth which is on the wing in May and June. The larva, which is squat in appearance and yellow with black spots, feeds on Bird's-foot Trefoil and related plants; it makes a hardened, oval cocoon on plant stems. The very similar-looking SIX-SPOT BURNET (*Z. filipendulae*) has six red spots on its forewing instead of five.

Common Forester *Adscita statices*
Wingspan 25mm

An attractive little day-flying moth, related to the burnets. The forewing is green and burnished with a bright, metallic sheen. The hindwing is pale and dull and is usually concealed when the moth is resting or feeding. Widespread but rather scattered in its distribution. In Britain, it is far from common, despite its English name; it occurs in England and Wales but is never more than locally common. Preferred habitats include damp meadows where the larval foodplant, sorrel, grows. The moths are most active on sunny days and are extremely fond of visiting the flowers of Ragged Robin.

Syntomis phegea Wingspan 35mm

A very distinctive day-flying moth. Although it is superficially similar to the burnet moths, it is not related to this group and may even recall a sawfly or solitary wasp at first glance. The upperwings are dark purplish-blue with a sheen in bright light; they bear largish white dots. The body of the moth is relatively long and narrow; it is bluish-green with two yellow bands. Occurs widely in central, and parts of southern Europe although it is absent from Britain. It has rather sluggish flight and often sits around on flower heads or on grasses on hot, sunny days. It favours grassy meadows, sometimes at reasonable altitudes, and flies from June to August.

139

Further reading

Carter, D. and Hargreaves, B., *Field Guide to Caterpillars in Britain and Europe*. Collins, London, 1986

Chinery, M. (Ed), *New Generation Guide: Butterflies and Day-flying Moths of Britain and Europe*. Collins, London, 1989

Goodden, R., *British Butterflies: A Field Guide*. David & Charles, Newton Abbot, 1978

Goodden, R. *Green Guide Butterflies of Britain and Europe*. New Holland (Publishers) Ltd, London, 1992

Higgins, L. and Hargreaves, B., *Field Guide to Butterflies of Britain and Europe*. Collins, London, 1983

Skinner, B. and Wilson, D., *Colour Identification Guide to the Moths of the British Isles*. Viking, London, 1984

Thomas. J., *Guide to Butterflies of the British Isles*. Royal Society for Nature Conservation, Lincoln, 1986

Useful addresses

Amateur Entomologist's Society
22 Salisbury Road, Feltham, Middlesex TW13 5DP

British Entomological and Natural History Society
74 South Audley Street, London W1Y 5FF

Butterfly Conservation
PO Box 22, Dedham, Essex CO7 6EY

English Nature
Northminster House, Peterborough PE1 1UA

The National Trust
36 Queen Anne's Gate, London SW1H 9AB

Royal Entomological Society of London
41 Queen's Gate, London SW7 5HR

The Wildlife Trusts (Royal Society for Nature Conservation)
The Green, Witham Park, Waterside South, Lincoln LN5 7JR

Worldwide Fund for Nature
Weyside Park, Godalming, Surrey GU7 1XR

Index

141

143